Good Housekeeping Book of
Home Decoration

Good Housekeeping

Book of
Home Decoration

MARY L. BRANDT

Prepared under the supervision of

MARY KRAFT
Director of the Good Housekeeping
Decorating Studio and Building Forum

McGraw-Hill Book Company, Inc.

NEW YORK   TORONTO   LONDON

Foreword

A "recipe" for a successful room is quite different from a recipe for a layer cake for which you can find all the ingredients in the kitchen cupboard. First, whether you are a bride or an established homemaker, you already have a collection of possessions which are different from anyone else's. These possessions, whether a few family heirlooms or some brand-new wedding presents, are the nucleus of your home. It is around such possessions that you will build your own individual decorative scheme. These are the things which give meaning and individuality to your home as you continue to choose and add other furnishings.

This book will help you to develop your taste and discrimination, to build confidence in your judgment, and to release your imagination so that you can best express your personality—and the composite personality of your family—in your surroundings. It will help you to make your house a home which gives comfort and pleasure to your family and your friends.

This book is mainly a picture book because, in decorating, a picture is indeed worth a thousand words. Here you will find pictures of many kinds of rooms in various styles of decoration, all suited to today's patterns of living; pictures of rooms we have designed or selected from the work of well-known decorators to illustrate the basic principles of interior decoration.

As you study these pages, certain rules will begin to emerge and repeat themselves. You will note good *scale*, which means the relation of the size of one object to other objects, and to the area in which it is placed. The importance of *proportion*, which refers to the relationship of each part of an object to its other parts, will become apparent. You will observe that *line*, which is the profile of an object, must be pleasing and graceful. And, all important, you'll begin to understand *color* and how it is used. You will find solutions that you can apply to your own problems, remembering that the most effective rooms are often the simplest.

It is our fervent desire and objective in the Decorating Studio of *Good Housekeeping* to offer guidance and inspiration to our readers in the creation of attractive, comfortable, and livable homes.

We believe that good homemaking and good decorating go hand in hand. And that a home where there is a serene, cheerful atmosphere, comfort and a sense of order, cannot help but be a warm and friendly place.

Mary Kraft

Contents

1 The Personal Approach to Your Home

The decoration and furnishing of a home is a rewarding experience —whether it's a house or an apartment, small or large, old or new; whether you already own most of your furnishings, only a few, or none at all; whether you've a small budget or unlimited funds. Each situation has its own set of problems, and each in its own way presents a challenge to your ingenuity and taste.

"But what is taste?" you ask.

In the final analysis, taste is choice. You may like quite a few different kinds of things, but in decorating your house you exercise your taste in choosing the things that are suitable in style, color, and scale, and that are practical and will go with things you already own. Some people have an instinctive gift for combining all these elements with pleasing results, just as some people can play complicated music by ear. But even gifted persons must study fundamentals of their art; and anyone, gifted or not, can cultivate understanding and appreciation of the tasteful and harmonious.

Treasured unusual possessions give a room individuality. The lovely screen has a Chinese design worked in needlepoint to keynote an entire room. Because of its durable nature, it will last for many years.

The ultimate aim in decorating is to express personal taste. Photostatic copies of old engravings blown up to nearly life size and pasted to screen panels make an eye-catching bit of unusual décor in the modern room.

Decorating demands more imagination and thought than money. A handsome and unusual "picture" fabric, repeated on an armchair, pillows, and in dramatic panels on a screen give this room an individual touch.

Make your hall personal and meaningful. In this quaint entry hall, flagstone flooring and the wallpaper pattern depicting antique automobiles set the mood of informality.

Plan your decoration around the way you live. Reclaimed mellow brick underscores the delightful dining room. The big brick fireplace is painted white. An oval braided rug repeats the table's shape and adds a homey note.

Most women learn in their teens the basic rules of dress and make-up, at least as applied to themselves. They learn, sometimes by trial and error, what colors and lines look best on them. They learn to recognize and to appreciate the worth of classic styles as the backbone of a wardrobe, and how to set them off with well-chosen accessories. They learn to resist the blandishments of gadgety bits that add nothing but confusion. They learn to be wary of the wildfire fashion that soon everyone and her sister will be wearing.

You can apply many of these same principles to your house. Begin by learning all you can about classic styles and study what was considered the best of yesterday. Try to see some of the period rooms in museums, and visit historic houses, including such authentic

4

Use your personal belongings as a starting point. In this charming bedroom, the distinctive wall-paper, reminiscent of an older pattern, and the random rag carpet are in keeping with the quaint chair-back headboards and old-fashioned chest with white marble top. Simple waffleweave cotton bedspreads harmonize with the old-fashioned furnishings.

restorations as Colonial Williamsburg. Books and magazines will be a great help, too, and well-done model rooms in the better stores will help you train your eye and give you a chance to study furniture arrangements and color schemes at first hand. If you live in a large city where big estates and collections are auctioned off from time to time, you can learn a lot about styles and periods by going to the pre-sale exhibition and studying the pieces with the help of the catalogue. The auction itself may be fun to attend, but be careful; an auction can be a trap for the inexperienced buyer who may get carried away by the excitement.

Reflect your personal tastes. An unusual collection of apothecary jars and other old-fashioned drugstore equipment give the modern living room a charming, friendly touch.

In this modern living room, long, low planks painted in a smart black and white harlequin pattern and mounted on brass legs draw attention to the collection of paintings hung to form a large over-all composition on the wall above.

Once you understand the rules of symmetry and balance by which the eighteenth century lived, you'll know better when and whether you may ignore them in your own twentieth-century décor. Even if you think of yourself as an out and out modernist, you'll find there are fundamentals to be learned here too. In studying the pictures of modern rooms in magazines and books and looking at model rooms, you'll come to appreciate the value of contrast in color and texture, the effectiveness of a plain background as a foil for a single rich ornament, the emotional necessity for hidden balance no matter how asymmetrical your room appears.

Mix the old with the new. A stunning black and white renaissance design contributes pattern to a den—guest room to make a perfect background for simple, graceful contemporary furniture.

▼ *A conversation group created around a small sofa with a slipcover made from an appliquéd quilt, a bright color note in the quaint, country living room pictured here.*

The development of taste is a progressive art; as you learn more you will find you have a greater appreciation and surer choice. You'll make some mistakes of course, or you'll outgrow some of your early enthusiasms. But you'll soon find that you won't be confused and unable to decide among a dozen things you admire; you'll be able to put your finger immediately on the thing that is right for you and the situation.

Decorating at its best is a personal art. It is decidedly not a matter of spending a lot of money. More important are imagination, the principles of good taste, and the utilization of those principles in terms of your personality and that of your family. The furnishings and decorations you choose and the way you use them are hallmarks that will make your home different from any other—a home that is attractive, comfortable, and a constant joy to live in.

▲ *The imprint of the personal touch is expressed in this charming, countrified living room. Subtle solid colors in carpet and sofas act as a foil for the unusual arrangement of old prints and quaint carved figure on the fireplace wall and the collection of interesting accessories.*

◀ *A den or television room gains popularity every year. Naturally this means convertible furniture, and this gay, informal furniture is an attractive case in point. The modern twin sofas turn into comfortable beds for overnight guests.*

▲ *Be different: use tints and shades of your favorite color again and again to give a room a serene and integrated feeling. In this charming living room, tints and shades of blue-green are echoed in walls, carpet, pillows, and decorative objects. Accent color is tangerine in sofa.*

2 Color Comes First

Color is one of the most important elements in decorating. The colors you want in your home are your own personal affair and should express your personal tastes and those of your family.

Some people have a natural talent for choosing and combining harmonious colors, but most of us need a little schooling in the simple basic principles of color. Once you understand these principles, you will find that working with color is fascinating.

What Is a Good Color Scheme?

The term *color scheme* simply means combining colors that go well together. But every good color scheme must have variety and interest —something dark, something light; something dull and something bright.

The first step in planning a color scheme is to choose the colors that please you and your family. You'll achieve best results if you keep your color scheme simple and use no more than three or four colors. A good rule to follow is to choose one or two relatively muted dominant colors for the largest areas such as walls, ceiling, floor covering, draperies, and large upholstered furniture, and one or two bright colors for the smallest areas such as seat pads, pillows, small occasional chairs, and accessories.

The color scheme should be appropriate for the room you are decorating. For example, if you have a north living room or a room having little sunlight and French provincial or countrified furniture, a predominantly warm color scheme, such as mustard yellow, citron yellow, and muted brown, enlivened by a contrasting cool color like turquoise, would create a warm, informal atmosphere.

The easiest and surest way to arrive at a color scheme and to avoid costly mistakes is to work out your ideas with color samples.

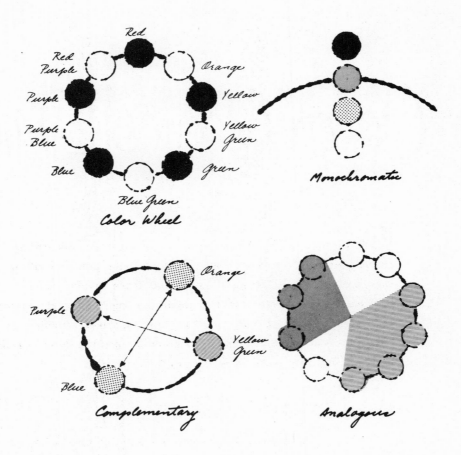

Color Wheel — Red, Orange, Yellow, Yellow Green, Green, Blue Green, Blue, Purple Blue, Purple, Red Purple

Monochromatic

Complementary — Orange, Yellow Green, Blue, Purple

Analogous

These may be magazine illustrations, swatches of material or wallpaper, or paint manufacturers' color chips. Cut each sample to a size proportionate to the area that it is to represent. The wall sample should be the largest one; the ceiling and floor samples next in size; the drapery and upholstery samples still smaller; and the accent colors the smallest of all. Place the wall, ceiling, and drapery samples on the upper half of a piece of white paper and the floor-covering sample on the lower half. Then arrange the upholstery and slip-cover samples and the accent colors in between them. Be sure to leave a white space around each sample. In this way, they will be placed somewhat as you would see them in your room.

Once you have worked out the color scheme you want with color samples, your shopping will be easier because you will know exactly what to look for. But don't expect the actual samples of materials to match your paper samples exactly, because the colors will be affected by the different textures of the surfaces.

In order to work out color schemes that please you and your family, you should know something about the characteristics of color itself and the three well-tried color systems.

▲ *In this small modern living room a warm analogous color scheme contrasts with the green trees outside. Warm whites blended with different shades of muted brown are accented with bright nasturtium and yellow in pillows, ceiling, and unique contemporary stove. Black accents in furniture and stove add a strong, dark note in the room.*

15

Accented with black, white is used throughout for unity in the modern living room shown here. Bright splashes of orange and yellow and unusual accessories give it warmth and an individuality all its own.

The Three Color Groups

Most of us at one time or another have seen a color wheel made up of the twelve basic colors. These twelve colors are divided into three color groups or families: *primary*, *secondary*, and *tertiary* colors.

Primary colors. First in importance are the primary pigment colors —red, yellow, and blue. They are basic because they cannot be produced by mixing any other colors. All other colors are mixtures of these three colors in various proportions.

Secondary colors. If equal parts of any two primary colors are combined, you get new colors referred to as the *secondary* colors. There are three secondary colors: green, orange, and purple.

Tertiary colors. Then if you mix equal parts of primary and secondary colors, you get six *tertiary* colors—yellow-green, blue-green, blue-purple, red-purple, red-orange, and yellow-orange.

Three Terms That Describe Color

The three terms that describe any given color are *hue*, *value*, and *intensity*.

Hue is merely another word for color. We say, for example, that any red, whether brilliant, dull, light, or dark, is a red hue.

Value refers to the lightness or darkness of a color—that is, how close it is to white at one end of the scale or black at the other end. Light colors that approach white are called *tints*. Conversely, those approaching black are called *shades*. A familiar example of a tint is that resulting if white is added to red; we may call this value rose or pink, depending on the proportion of white to red.

Intensity refers to the degree of brilliance of a color. A color may be of high intensity, say a vivid red-orange like an oriental poppy, or it may be of lower intensity, say a dull red-orange like a brick or a piece of terra cotta. Any color becomes dull or grayed when either black or its complementary color is added to it. Thus, if a little green is added to a brilliant red, the red becomes less intense. Or if black is added to red, it again becomes a muted shade.

It is very important to remember that colors of full intensity, such as brilliant orange, pure red, vivid blue, are exciting and fatigue the eye. For this reason they should generally be used only in small areas in a room. Dull or grayed colors (lower intensity), such as misty blue, olive green, or warm beige, are best for large areas.

A proper balance of values and intensities of colors will best be achieved in your color scheme if you use no more than two slightly different colors in different values (from light to dark) in the largest areas, and bright accent colors in the smallest areas. For example toast-colored upholstery, a muted-brown rug, beige curtains, and pumpkin as the accent color for small areas would be less intense against sandalwood walls than against blue-green walls, because any color seems less intense if used with a similar neighboring color.

How to Recognize Differences in Color

All of the many different colors in home-furnishings merchandise have descriptive color names from season to season, as lime, pumpkin, aqua, lilac, celadon green, and so on, but the basic color names never change.

If you are able to recognize the twelve basic colors and their different values and intensities, it will help you immeasurably when you are working out a color scheme.

◀ *A monochromatic color scheme of blues, ranging from midnight blue to lighter blues, gives this informal provincial living room great distinction.*

▼ *White accented with black is a foil for a collection of antique Bristol-blue accessories in this handsome contemporary bedroom.*

▲ *Black and white keys this traditional living room that expresses a comfortable new formality. A rich red (on upholstered chair) adds a warm accent to dominant black and white flooring and checked chair pads.*

A mixture of different styles of furniture and accessories adapts to an analogous color scheme of blue and blue-green in this modern living room. Antique white walls give a spacious look to the room.

An Ideal Setting
For Family
Relaxation

▲ *For a cool serene look, use blue or green and white. In this pretty living room different shades of blue, as well as large areas of white, give the room a refreshing, cool look. Yellow accents add a contrasting color to an otherwise monochromatic color scheme.*

▼ *Give your bedroom fresh appeal by using tints and shades of one color. A charming bed–sitting room, done in tints and shades of luscious pinks and reds, is highlighted by elegant patterned draperies and deep triple-looped swag in tints and shades of pink. This classic window treatment is a romantic note in an otherwise contemporary setting.*

A contrasting color scheme of light blue and gold, taken from the printed fabric, gives the living room (above) an air of elegance. Tawny beige acts as a foil for contrasting orange and green in modern room (below). Analogous colors ranging from green to blue to blue-green give the country living room (opposite page) great individuality. Black and white coupled with yellow gives the modern room (opposite) a fresh, crisp look. Pink and sharp green give the ladylike bedroom (opposite) a vital new look.

▲ *Turquoise, yellow, and green printed linen slipcovers establish the color scheme in this living room. Green grasscloth walls make a cool, restful background for the bright draperies and yellow armchair.*

Wall-to-wall carpeting can be the dramatic color contrast in an otherwise monochromatic color scheme. This all-green living room uses a deep-cut pile carpet in gold to set off the traditional furniture. In the dining room on the opposite page, with table, chairs, and sideboard in an American provincial design, the graceful "Pomegranate Tree" mural-type wallpaper contributes decorative interest. It is also the inspiration for the yellow-and-white monochromatic color scheme. White is the dominant color, accented with yellow in chair pads, flowers, and accessories.

▲ *Tints and shades of red and red-orange, such as pinky beige, muted brick-red, pinks, and rosy-red, make a pleasing analogous color scheme for this cozy countrified living room.*

▶ *White works wonders with any period or color. As a background, white gives a spacious look to this small bed–sitting room. Color accents of turquoise in ceiling, pillows, and hard flooring, and the black in the daybed covers look much sharper used against white.*

It isn't difficult to train your eye to recognize these differences in color if you try a very simple game of color matching. Pick out several small samples of colors—some light, some dark, some dull (or grayed), and some bright. They may be fabric swatches, bits of yarn and ribbon, or other small colored samples you can carry in your handbag. When you see a flower, a hat, a book cover, or any other colored object you think matches one of your samples, take it out and check it.

As you continue to match your color samples with those you find along the way, you will soon find that your awareness of color has become more acute.

The Three Color Systems

To attain real mastery in the area of color, you should have a working knowledge of the three well-tried systems of color combinations. A knowledge of these systems will make it easier for you to assemble the colors for your room schemes.

But first you must know what a color wheel is. This device is a circular color chart on which, for convenience, the colors are evenly spaced (see illustration, page 14). Yellow appears at the top of the circle followed counterclockwise by yellow-orange, orange, orange-red, red, red-purple, to purple (at the bottom of the circle) and then through purple to blue-purple, blue, blue-green, green, yellow-green, back to yellow.

The use of a color wheel will help you visualize the three most-used color systems. They are *complementary*, *analogous*, and *monochromatic* color schemes.

Complementary Color Schemes

Colors that are opposite one another on the wheel are called *complementary* colors. When complementary colors are combined in a variety of tints, shades, and degrees of intensity, the effect is usually vigorous and lively.

True complementary colors are red and green, red-orange and blue-green, orange and blue, yellow-orange and blue-violet, and yellow and violet.

However, many color schemes are composed not of true complementary colors—those diametrically opposite one another on the color wheel—but of colors located at any point on opposite sides of the color wheel. A color scheme of this kind might have soft orange walls, more intense red-orange upholstery, beige casement curtains, and tawny-beige carpet (light yellow-orange), with bright leaf-green accents (slightly yellowish-green) in small areas.

30

▲ *In this formal, classic dining room, yellow and white striped draperies and canopied valance, at window, afford a pleasant color contrast for the predominant color, soft blue, in walls and furniture.*

Analogous Color Schemes

An *analogous* color scheme is one composed of colors located side by side or close to one another on the wheel.

Analogous color schemes are usually more subtle and restful than complementary color schemes. To make them interesting, you must use various light tints and various dark shades of the colors you choose.

A typical analogous color scheme for a modern hall might consist of pale beige walls (a light tint of yellow-orange), a dull or grayed orange carpet with a brownish cast, and bright pomegranate (intense red-orange) accents.

▼ *Interesting use of different materials, as textured carpeting, wallpaper, brick, quarry tile, flooring, and wood paneling, makes a distinctive background for this living room and kitchen-dining room. Over-all color scheme of natural wood tones and turquoise ties areas together.*

Monochromatic Color Schemes

A *monochromatic*, or one-hue, color scheme is one made up of tints and shades of a single color. Monochromatic color schemes are more difficult to work out than one might think because they tend to create a monotonous effect. Both variety in values and intensities of the color, and unusual designs and textures, can be utilized to avoid monotony.

Once you understand the principles of colors and their combinations in the three color systems, don't be too concerned about them. Use them only as a guide. The illustrations in this book show good examples of different kinds of color schemes; you might like to adapt some of these to your own decorating plans.

Above all, don't forget that repetitions of any one of these three color harmonies can be used as linking colors in adjacent rooms. This treatment is especially effective in the entrance hall, living room, and dining room. For example, you might decorate your hall with a scenic wallpaper having a background the same color as the paint on your living-room walls, and paper your dining room with a tone-on-tone pattern, such as damask or stripes, in darker and lighter values of one of the colors of the scenic wallpaper in the hall.

And finally, the selection of color for any room is generally determined by the light and exposure—whether it faces south, north, east, or west. In a room with a southern exposure, or one with a western exposure that gets lots of afternoon sunlight, cool, restful colors such as blues, blue-greens, and greens are best suited.

For rooms with a northern exposure, or with an eastern exposure where the sunlight is present for only a few hours in the morning, warm colors, such as yellows, pinks, or light tints of orange and red-orange, offset the coldness.

▶

Instead of using true complementary colors of red-orange and blue-green in this living room, the predominant color, red-orange, in muted brick-patterned wallpaper, bright velvet-covered love-seat, and abstract design in carpet, is accented with green, shown on armchair.

3 Planning the Living Room

The living room of today is planned so that all members of the family, as well as their friends, can enjoy the many activities that now take place in this area. The first step, then, in planning furnishings for your living room is to decide how you will use the room and how it will be used by different members of your family.

The second step is to decide what kind of furnishings will create the atmosphere you want. A tasteful, friendly living room must have comfortable, useful furniture in consistent and balanced groupings, cheerful colors, proper lighting, and well-chosen accessories.

◄

Groupings of low, comfortable furniture make this roof-high modern living-dining room seem more spacious. Over-all carpet ties areas together.

If you want to achieve an elegant, formal effect in your living room, some of these styles should appeal to you. Formal furnishings most used today—either antiques or good reproductions—are styles of the eighteenth and early nineteenth centuries of England, France, and Italy. English eighteenth-century furniture designs with which you may be familiar are Chippendale, Hepplewhite, Sheraton, and Adam. Popular French eighteenth-century designs are those of the Louis XV and Louis XVI periods. Classic furniture styles of the early nineteenth century are the English Regency designs, the Directoire and the Empire styles of France and Italy, and the Biedermeir style of Germany and Austria.

If you prefer an informal, casual living room, there are several appropriate treatments. You can achieve a quaint country look by using such styles of the past as early American and French provincial; or you may like to mix provincial and modern styles. But for an uncluttered look, simple modern furniture is most effective. You can even combine modern wood pieces with outdoor-indoor metal and rattan furniture.

Or, for a semiformal atmosphere, combine one or two important formal pieces, such as a Louis XV fruitwood chest and a pair of painted Louis XV chairs, with simple modern furniture.

Large-scaled contemporary furniture and restraint in colors, window treatment, and accessories give this old-fashioned, high-ceilinged living room a modern look.

This delightful one-room apartment is furnished almost entirely with pieces picked up in second-hand shops and refinished or reupholstered. Shutters used at windows and as cupboard doors came from a dismantled house. Coffee table got a new Formica top. The pretty color scheme and attractive accessories give the room great individuality.

Changes in floor level in this modern house create various points of view of the delightful landscape seen through the window.

The entrance to the light-filled living room (left) is from an elevated hall (below). Traditional furniture blends well with modern background of stone, wood, and glass.

▲ *A monochromatic color scheme of orange, in this contemporary living-dining room, is accented by white walls, black upholstery, coffee table, lamps, and dining chairs. The orange-and-gold-patterned draperies are repeated on the loveseat. Dining table and spindle-back dining chairs are separated from the kitchen by a room divider.*

▲ *Spaciousness and restful comfort are achieved in this small modern living-room area by an asymmetrical arrangement of low furniture around the off-center fireplace. The sofa and coffee table (in foreground), placed horizontally in front of fireplace, act as room divider between dining el and living room.*

If you like to entertain a lot, a way to accommodate a large group of people in minimum space is a wall-long bench with padded seat, as shown in this modern living-dining room. The built-in padded backrest neatly turns a corner; a matching bench forms an additional seat. There's plenty of space for a crowd to eat buffet supper and watch television comfortably.

▶

This comfortable modern living room is rather small, but the arrangement of two daybeds along one wall, with storage chest in between, makes it seem more spacious. Tailored bolsters, at ends and backs of daybeds, give the illusion of sofas by day. The decorative wall treatment of snapshots mounted alike adds a personal, individual touch.

▲

A modern living-dining room can accommodate overnight guests; couch turns into a bed. The room divider gives an illusion of two rooms. Interesting grouping of accessories adds interest.

In this attractive living room, the bold plaid in tones of pink, charcoal, and turquoise suggests the color scheme for the entire room. It is also perfectly at home with the countrified furniture of French provincial inspiration. An over-all composition of odd-sized pictures and decorative clock makes an interesting focal point for the conversation grouping of furniture.

◀

▶

Simplicity and individuality are the hallmarks that make this living room distinctive. A monochromatic scheme of soft gold tones makes a restrained background for books, pictures, and decorative accessories. Eighteenth-century table serves as desk and lamp table.

When you have decided how you will use the room, the atmosphere you want, and the kind of furniture you need, make a decorating plan of the elements for the room in the following order:

1. Over-all color scheme—dominant colors and accent colors
2. Wall treatment—paint, wallpaper, or both
3. Floor covering—wall-to-wall carpet, room-size rug, or hard flooring with area rugs
4. Window treatment—draperies, curtains, or both
5. Fabrics for upholstery and slipcovers
6. Lamps and lighting

7. Smart accessories—pictures, pillows, ashtrays, flower containers.

Above all, use restraint in the selection of colors, furniture, fabrics, and accessories; keep it simple. Be sure that what you choose is suitable for the room and that the furnishings are well proportioned.

It is not always easy to achieve a sense of order and balance in the small present-day living rooms because so many of them have irregular shapes or limited wall space, off-center fireplaces, and large window areas. To make it easier for you to arrange furniture groups, here are a few suggestions. First, decide where each grouping of furniture will be placed according to its particular use (a television grouping, a conversation grouping, a game grouping). Plan the furniture groupings so that they won't interfere with traffic to doors. Then place the large pieces of furniture first. They should be placed either parallel with a wall or window or at right angles, never diagonally. After you have placed the large pieces, the small ones such as lamp tables and occasional chairs will fall into place in relation to them.

The Living-Dining Room

The most important point about a living-dining room, where the furniture groupings must take care of all family activities, including dining, is that to achieve an orderly and uncluttered look, much of the furniture must do double duty—for example, a table to be used for dining, writing, and playing games; dining chairs that can be used as extra seating; storage pieces for things used in both the living and dining areas. It is often particularly helpful to use the dining area for more than one purpose—as a combination dining-television area, or a place to do your family mending and sewing.

In these pages you'll see many ideas for furnishing living rooms and living-dining rooms.

▲ *In this provincial dining room, a ready-made corner
cabinet with louvered doors, designed to harmonize
with either French or American furnishings, houses
a television set.*

▲ *A room planned for the happy mixture of prized possessions is expressed in this cozy provincial living room. The focal point is an impressive table, composed of a huge brass tray, set on a ready-made metal tubing base.*

◄

Make a bay window the focal point in your room. In this old-fashioned living room, the handsome toile de jouy *draperies framing the bay window emphasize the French-provincial feeling of the furniture.*

49

The One-room Apartment

If you're just getting started in a one-room apartment, a careful plan for the furnishings and their arrangement is a necessity because every inch must count. Start with the largest pieces—the sleeping units, storage units, and large table for dining and work. If you haven't room for a sizable dining table, look for an adjustable coffee table, a table with drop leaves, or a console-type table that may be extended. Place your dining grouping as close to the kitchen area as possible.

Wall Treatments

Today there are all kinds of unusual materials to use on walls. Exotic woods, glass, fabric, mural-type scenic wallpapers, and interesting construction materials are only a few examples of what can be used to create attractive, dramatic interiors.

You might, for example, accent one wall in your living room as a strong contrast. If your living room is modern in feeling, you might use brick, or a simulated plastic brick on the entire fireplace wall, or wood paneling; or, paint one wall a bright color and break it up in the center with a decorative wall treatment.

The use of only one solid color for walls allows greater freedom in your selection of colors for other things in the room. Moreover, solid-colored walls make the best background for your furnishings. Light-colored walls tend to make a room seem larger; nonetheless a definite color that harmonizes with the other colors in your room will be more effective than a "safe," commonplace color like cream or a washed-out green that you have been told "will go with everything."

Generally, the woodwork is painted the same color as the walls. If your walls are a light color such as sky-blue or pale beige, a ceiling the same color or just a trifle lighter will give an effect of unity. For a dramatic effect, paint the ceiling a different color from the walls, but one that harmonizes with the other colors in the room—for instance, frosty-white walls with a turquoise ceiling that ties in with turquoise-upholstered chairs and accessories.

▲ *A serene color scheme of tints and shades of green, blue-green, and blue, taken from the floral print on sofa, chairs, and ottoman, helps to integrate the happy mixture of traditional and modern furniture and accessories in this attractive living room.*

▲ *Striking decoration is often achieved by using an overscaled design. A lovely grillwork paper adds an elegant touch to this traditional living room. Beautifully scaled, it provides an interesting but unobtrusive background for pictures.*

Today's wallpaper is more than just a pretty pattern on the wall. The wide variety of such unusual designs as gay florals, stripes, modern patterns, repeat scenics, damasks, neat, evenly spaced designs, and textured finishes makes possible an astonishing number of interesting effects.

Architectural defects such as juts in the walls and broken-up areas can be disguised by using a small allover design or a pronounced textured pattern. A scenic wallpaper or one that simulates a Japanese Shoji screen can give depth and an illusion of space to a small room.

Floor Coverings

Today carpets are available in a wide variety of beautiful colors, interesting textures, and attractive designs at reasonable prices.

Some carpets and rugs are woven on a loom and some are made by a revolutionary new method called *tufting*. This consists of drawing yarns through a sturdy duck or jute backing. Most carpets and rugs now are laminated on the back with heavy latex. Also there is a greater variety of yarns used. Whether the carpet or rug is woven or tufted, you can make your selection from a wide range of textures. If you use a solid color, be sure the one you choose harmonizes with the other colors in your living room.

A wall-to-wall carpet will make a small room appear larger, especially if the color is a light one that matches or blends with the walls. Wall-to-wall carpeting also ties adjacent rooms together.

On a handsome polished floor one or more area rugs will help unite your furniture groupings. Today's area rugs are quite different from the old-fashioned small scatter rugs, not only because they are available in larger sizes, but also because they are made in various

◄

Even one touch of wallpaper, imaginatively used, can have a good effect. A fine traditional floral pattern, used in panels above the dado in this living room, conveys an air of elegance all its own. The design of pinks and reds on a blue background is the inspiration for the color scheme in the room.

53

shapes, colors, textures, and designs, including handmade rugs of all kinds from all over the world. You can now purchase relatively inexpensive rugs—some sculptured, some textured, and some with designs. However, you'll see in the illustrations that many floors are so decorative and handsome that they do not need rugs.

Many of the attractive carpets and rugs on the market are inexpensive, ranging from braided, hooked, and some tufted rugs, to well-styled fiber and straw rugs.

Window Treatments

The right kind of curtains can make any window attractive, but the modern trend favors simplicity. Your window treatment can be handled as part of the background and appear to melt into the wall, or it may be made an important decorative feature. In any case, it should be simple in effect (see illustrations).

In almost every room, there is some problem about how to treat certain windows. Narrow windows can be widened by hanging the curtains a few inches out on the walls on either side of the window. If the picture window in your living room is near the ceiling, curtains hung from a ceiling track to the floor will give the room more height. The problem posed by a picture window and a glass door unevenly balanced on the same wall can be made a decorative asset by curtaining the entire wall space, from ceiling to floor, to unify and dramatize this area. Curtains can frame a beautiful view or conceal a dull one.

Café curtains, by virtue of their versatility, can be used in many interesting ways: hung at midwindow length, they give a narrow living room the appearance of greater width; hung in tiers, they make a charming window treatment for an informal, provincial living room, or will solve the problem of a window with a radiator beneath it.

For an elegant, formal look in your living room, hang valances, either shaped or festooned, over floor-length curtains.

▲

Mellow pine paneling, selected in random widths, makes a warm background for figurines, ceramics, and old Chinese painting in this comfortable living room. The fireplace is of painted white brick, flush with the walls in the modern manner.

▶

Contemporary color scheme of orange, pink, and black makes a dramatic background for painted Venetian furniture in this elegant living room. Handsome wallpaper border adds a distinctive touch.

◀ *A skillful selection and arrangement of a few important accessories, of right proportions and character, give the classic Sheraton table personality. The bowl of flowers adds a charming note.*

▼ *Elegant and unusual accessories are the major color accents and decorative features in this formal but comfortable living room with a skillful mixture of eighteenth-century French furniture, and contemporary upholstered pieces.*

▲ *In perfect harmony with the restrained atmosphere of an eighteenth-century living room is the handsome paneling above the fireplace and the paneled doors faintly outlined with light Bristol-blue. The muted-gold rug is a perfect foil for the brighter Bristol-blue in furniture, accessories, and trimming on draperies and shaped valance.*

▲ *A rug in a handsome Moorish design contributes pattern and inspiration for color scheme in this white-walled living room with a mixture of modern and traditional furniture. The red-orange, brown, and gold tones in the rug are repeated in furniture, draperies, and accessories.*

▼ *The stunning rug in this modern living room is an example of the individuality you can achieve in a custom-made rug. Composed of rectangles in shades of green and brown and of different pile heights, it was inspired by an abstract painting and provides all the design necessary. With a little ingenuity, you can create a similar effect by making a hooked rug in tints and shades of related colors to harmonize with your room scheme.*

◀ *The textured area rug in woven striped effect, with a glint of metallic yarn, is used for contrast with the elegant antique furniture and polished parquet floor in this living room.*

A handsome modern-primitive design in shades of blue, gold, and olive on an off-white background underscores the comfortable conversation grouping in this contemporary living room and suggests color scheme for room. ▶

▼ *A fireplace wall of brick- and wood-paneled walls makes a warm and cozy background for this inviting living room. Contemporary upholstered furniture, combined with a traditional wing chair, forms a comfortable grouping in front of the fireplace.*

4 Dining Rooms

Not too many years ago, the dining room in even modest homes was a stilted, impersonal room used only at mealtime. In many respects it replaced the old-fashioned parlor as an emblem of social status. Today there are no set rules about how a dining room should be arranged and furnished; it depends on your requirements for the activities that take place in your dining room. For example, it may serve as a multipurpose room, such as a television-dining room. On the other hand, if you entertain a great deal, you may prefer the formality of a separate dining room. But remember that the primary requirements for today's dining room are comfort, attractiveness, and charm.

Once you have decided on the kind of dining room that will meet your own requirements, make a plan for the specific pieces of furniture you will need before you go shopping.

Furniture Arrangements

Since there are no longer rules about the arrangement of furniture in a separate dining room, when you make a plan for the furniture, think in terms of the actual pieces you will need for the places you are going to put them. You will need a good-looking table, preferably expandable for large sit-down dinners and buffet suppers; a storage piece for linens and silver; chairs, either matching or nonmatching. (A combination of matching small upholstered host and hostess chairs with wooden side chairs would be acceptable.) When not in use for dining, upholstered chairs could be used in the living room for extra seating.

◀

The focal point in this dining area is a large hanging shelf filled with a collection of old china, figurines, books, and pictures.

63

If the window in your dining room overlooks a lovely garden, place the table and chairs in front of the window with the table either parallel with or at right angles to the window, depending on its length. If your dining room is to be used for family activities other than dining, such as study and work, look for storage units that include a desk arrangement and possibly a space for books, and place the dining table and chairs against one wall or in front of the window.

For a small dining room, choose furniture that is scaled to the room. If your dining room is large and rather formal, consider using a small extra table, perhaps in front of the window. It could be a drop-leaf table or a small console table to be opened when it is used for breakfast and informal lunch.

▲ An unusual rug gives this contemporary dining room an identity all its own. The strong turquoise accent in the rug is picked up in draperies and a pair of ceramic birds on the chest. The modern pineapple candle sconces are the rust color of the background in the rug.

◄

Modern table and chairs at a new level—about 3 inches lower than normal height—are remarkably versatile and comfortable for informal entertaining, as shown in this dining area.

▲ *Instead of being used only at mealtimes, this pleasant, informal dining room, in simple early American vein, sees round-the-clock service as a place for games, study, work, and entertaining. The quaint wallpaper keynotes the color scheme of pink and beige. Pink is repeated in ceiling, checked curtains, braided rug, and china.*

▼ Especially dear to younger residents is the wonderful snack bar; this one is really a half brick wall separating the kitchen from the living-dining room. The bar makes serving breakfast or an informal lunch remarkably easy. One wall of kitchen is completely filled with pine storage cabinets; along another is housed a stove with old-fashioned hood. Pots and pans hang from walls to form part of decorating scheme.

Styles of Furniture

Although the dining room of the past almost always had a matching style of furniture, today the trend is toward mixing different styles. Mixing compatible styles will give your dining room more distinction and individuality. For example, if your preference is the eighteenth-century styles of England, you might mix eighteenth- and early-nineteenth-century pieces, such as a Sheraton pedestal table with English Regency chairs and an English Regency breakfront with brass grillwork doors. Or if you like modern furniture with a touch of traditional, you might combine an oval contemporary table with Italian provincial chairs and contemporary storage pieces.

Graceful "transitional" furniture, equally at home in contemporary or period settings, is used in this dining room against a bold block pattern. Accessories add a traditional note.

The intriguing wallpaper design of old watches on a muted orange background fits the spirit of the old combined with the new in this charming dining room.

▲ *The dining area in this living-dining room is also used for games. The walls, carpet, and chair pads repeat the yellow-greens and blue-greens in the printed draperies.*

A mixture of painted Louis XVI chairs with a Louis XVI table in a mellow wood finish gives this small dining area great distinction. Pale blue walls make it seem larger.

With an air of elegance, this dining room follows a new trend; Regency furniture is used against a colorful wallpaper instead of a simple, classic background. The handsome traditional design of the wallpaper is repeated in matching draperies.

Cork, because it is easy to care for, makes an ideal floor for a modern dining room. Here, it also keynotes the color scheme; its glowing tones are reflected in the mural hung above a simulated brick dado.

The lovely Spanish patterned rug keynotes the color scheme in this handsome traditional dining room. Yellow tones appear in striped wallpaper, dado, and chair seats; orange is repeated in draperies and valance.

Unusual treasured possessions give this traditional dining room individuality. One wonderful accessory, like the four-branched brass hurricane stand, casts a glow of formality over the simple table setting. The handsome painting over the buffet adds an elegant touch.

Color Schemes and Wall Treatments

Your dining room can be as colorful and gay as you want because it is the one room that should express cheer rather than repose. Since a dining room ought to be pleasing to many people of different tastes (your family and your friends), you will find that fresh, clear colors are more apt to put everybody in a happy mood.

If your dining room is a dark, cheerless room, a predominating warm color scheme, say of tints and shades of yellow or pink, will give it an intimate, friendly feeling. On the other hand, if the room is bright and sunny, tints and shades of blue, blue-green, or green will make it pleasant and cool. But cool colors usually need the sparkle of a warm accent color, such as daffodil-yellow or tangerine.

An important point to remember when you are planning a color scheme for your dining room is this: if it is adjacent to the living room and hall it ought to be linked to these rooms by the same color. Suppose, for example, that your sun-flooded living room has a color scheme of predominant blue-greens with accents of yellow and orange, and that your dining room is a dark, northern room. You might use tints and shades of the living-room accent colors, yellow and orange, as the predominating colors in the dining room. This will give the room a warm and sunny feeling (see page 72).

The dining room is one of the few places in your home where an unusual decorative effect is practical, because, since the room is in use only part of the time, you won't tire of it easily.

Solid-colored walls make a suitable background for old portraits, pictures, or a handsome mirror; if need be, they can be made interesting if you use a chair rail (dado) on the lower part of the walls, painted either a shade darker than the walls or a contrasting color. Another way of creating an unusual effect with paint is to use a different color on the ceiling. You might choose a soft, clear yellow, such as daffodil or citron-yellow, which will give the room a feeling of sunlight, or a cool color, such as azure-blue or aquamarine, to make a low ceiling seem higher.

If you want the walls to be the important decorative feature in your dining room and to tie in with a particular style of furniture, consider covering them with a handsome patterned wallpaper; or, you might frame the wallpaper in panels (see pages 69, 70, 80, 81).

If your dining room is small and you feel that a strongly patterned wallpaper on all four walls would "close in" the room too much, use this paper on only one or two walls and either paint the remaining ones or use a textured paper with a solid-colored effect, such as grasscloth, or one with a simulated woven effect. A wallpaper with

▼ *Floor-to-ceiling windows make dining area in this modern living-dining room light and airy and provide a pleasant view of terrace and trees. Green tones in foliage and trees predominate in room scheme.*

▲ *To give this traditional dining room individuality, tall screens with a patterned fabric stretched taut over frames are attached to each side of the window.*

Simple countrified furniture, quaint coin-dot wallpaper, colorful braided carpet, and unusual accessories give this informal dining room individuality and a friendly feeling. In the French-provincial dining room below, café curtains hung on brass rings, with swag forming draperies on each side, solve the problem of a window with a radiator beneath it.

a bold pattern, when used on one or two walls, is especially good
for a dining room because people spend relatively little time here,
and so are not likely to become fatigued by a strong pattern.

Even one touch of wallpaper imaginatively used can turn an ordinary dining room into a truly distinguished one. For example, an
elegant wallpaper border used around the top of the walls, and
covering the valances too, will add interest to a formal dining room
and give an architectural look to the windows. Tall narrow screens
covered with a patterned paper and placed on either side of a large
window might be the focal point in the dining room, or they could
camouflage uneven wall spaces on either side of the window (see
page 76).

Scenic papers or murals are especially suitable for dining rooms
(and halls too), because they give an illusion of spaciousness. What
could be more pleasant than eating amid pleasant scenery, such as
a Mediterranean coastline, a lovely garden view, a French provincial
country scene, or a vista of the Far East? In a small dining room even
only one wall covered with a scenic paper will help make the room
seem larger and give the illusion of a lovely view. Often, one or more
framed scenic panels, hung from the ceiling to the dado, serve as
distinctively as a painting that is hung over a chest or buffet.

Floor Coverings and Hard Flooring

With colorful, dramatic wallpaper, you can use a wall-to-wall carpet, a room-size rug in a bold color, hard flooring (in a two-toned
block effect, for example), or rubber, vinyl, or terrazzo with brass
inserts to give your dining room great style. If the walls and curtains
are unobtrusive, a patterned rug or one in an important solid color
(perhaps with a carved border design) in an interesting shape will
dramatize your floor.

▲ *The quaint wallpaper of scenes of old Salem, in tints and shades of blue and framed like pictures, keynotes the decorating theme in an early-American dining room. The coordinated drapery fabric has a patchwork pattern.*

◀

This small dining alcove is papered in a colorful carriage print. The design forms a bright background for white curtains and metal furniture. A carriage lamp repeats the theme.

▲ A simple rust and brown leaf-patterned wallpaper, in block form, makes a striking background for white woodwork in this early-American living-dining room.

Window Treatments

A colorful patterned curtain or plain fabric in an unusual treatment (such as ceiling-to-floor sheer casement curtains with an embroidered border or an attractive fringe outlining the edges) gives a dramatic effect. Or, hang cafe curtains in an original way, or treat the top of the curtains with an unusual shaped or festooned valance. (See page 77 for unusual window treatment.)

Accessories and Lighting

One beautiful or unusual object can be the dramatic focal point in your dining room. It might be a handsome screen, an important painting, an elegant old mirror, or a lovely flower arrangement. Or, an interesting collection of objects arranged on shelves might provide the center of interest.

General illumination and specific lighting for certain areas should be as carefully planned as lighting for the living room. General illumination could be built-in lighting, traditional units, or a combination of both. Specific lighting for the dining table and possibly the storage unit could be a combination of lighting such as: candlelight on the table and a lamp on the chest; a ceiling pulley lamp over the table with candlelight or a lamp on the chest; or a decorative ceiling fixture over the table.

▲ *Graceful pieces in early American tradition are perfectly scaled for a small dining room—study. They show to charming advantage against a contemporary design of butterflies on a sheer fabric.*

◀

Printed casement-cloth curtains contribute pattern to the windows in the dining area of this living-dining room and make a pleasant background for the sleek modern dining furniture.

This charming dining room would appeal to those who like the formality of the typical colonial style. Against soft blue-green walls, the crystal chandelier and candelabra play an important role. Attractive window niches provide room for a variety of accessories.

Dining Elsewhere in the House

The dining room however is only one of the rooms in which today's meals are served. The combination living-dining room found in so many new homes calls for a somewhat different approach to dining. New dual-purpose furniture has been developed to replace conventional dining-room furniture. For example, tables are now available that convert between meals to coffee tables or desks. Others can be expanded with either drop leaves or concealed leaves to be used as table-desks or work tables when not needed for meals. Dining room chairs are now designed to double as occasional chairs for extra seating in the living room. Modern storage chests are designed to fit into any room in the house.

The old-fashioned teacart has also come back in a new guise. This new cart-on-wheels often has drop leaves or expandable leaves, so that it can be used for both serving and dining.

There is a growing trend toward serving meals in still other parts of the house. Meals may be served in the kitchen, on the terrace, in the living room, on the sun porch, or in the family room. In good weather it's fun to eat out on the terrace or porch. You can now purchase metal, rattan, or canvas furniture, suitable for both living and dining activities, that can stay out all summer.

If you have a dining area in the kitchen, make it attractive enough to be a delightful place for family dinners and informal entertaining. If your kitchen is small, a built-in counter for dining leaves maximum space for working.

Naturally meals served in these areas are less formal than full-scale sit-down dinner in the dining room, but these meals need not be less attractive; the settings in which they are served deserve the same ingredients—color, imagination, and attention to details.

Table Settings

The most important feature about dining anywhere in your home is an attractive and colorful table with imaginative table appointments.

One of the easiest ways to vary your table settings is to introduce two (or even three) colors in table mats, cloths, and napkins. For example, you might use a sky-blue tablecloth on a round table, and a different color for napkins, such as citron-yellow, or you could alternate between citron-yellow and moss-green napkins at every other place setting. It is a good idea to keep on hand a supply of different colored table mats, cloths, and napkins that can be used interchangeably. A plentiful supply of interesting containers for fruit and flowers, potted plants and leaves, and several pairs of candlesticks are also a help in achieving variety.

Avoid buying commonplace matching candlesticks and bowls, for nowadays distinctive and interesting decorative arrangements are within your reach. There are all kinds of imaginative containers available at moderate prices, including baskets, tureens, mortars, pewter and earthenware bowls and mugs, and simple contemporary glass and ceramic bowls.

5 Halls

Whether you have a tiny foyer or a wide entrance hall, this area is most important. Here, visitors form their first impression of your home when they arrive and the last impression before they leave.

The welcome that your hall extends—not only to your friends but to your family as well—should certainly be as cordial as possible. The entrance hall is the one place where appearance is more important than utility; it should have a distinctive yet friendly feeling. This effect can be achieved easily by using an interesting floor treatment, an unusual wall treatment, a few inviting pieces of furniture, a few important accessories, and above all, an attractive color scheme.

When you plan your foyer or hall, think of how it will be used before you buy any furniture. You will need a place where guests can put small things, such as gloves and hats. The most useful piece of furniture is a console or a chest with a mirror over it, lighted on each side with wall brackets, a lamp or two, or overhead lighting. If there isn't a closet to hang up coats, you could use a small wall-type hat rack. It might be an old one, or one of the new modern ones, or you might use decorative brass hooks. If you have a large hall, an attractive bench or chairs will make it more comfortable and friendly and also provide a place for your guests and family to remove or put on snow boots and rubbers.

It is imperative, of course, to plan a color scheme for your hall that relates to the rooms adjacent to it, especially the living room, because you pass so quickly from the hall to the living room.

◄

Simple architectural details, interesting use of materials, and colorful abstract on glass in brass divider give this entry hall importance.

▲ *A long unbroken wall in a hall can provide convenient storage space.*
In this hall oriental-inspired chests are used for storage. Note inter-
esting arrangement of accessories, such as pewter on graduated shelves
and chest.

89

Formal Halls

If the furnishings in your living and dining rooms are formal in character, your entrance hall should be rather impersonal and elegant in feeling. Furniture that is formal in character, be it traditional, modern, or a mixture of styles, is most appropriate; it should be placed in balanced arrangements with a few important accessories. As an extension of the formal atmosphere, you might play up the floor with a handsome smooth-surface flooring with brass inserts, with one of the new elegant marble effects, or with a dense-piled wall-to-wall carpet. The most practical floor treatment is a smooth-surface flooring because, with one of the new wax finishes, it is resistant to soil and easier to clean than carpeting.

If you want to emphasize the walls, mural-type scenic paper will give your foyer or hall an illusion of space, or a bold design will make it look gay and interesting. If you paint the walls, consider a striking effect. For example, use a light color such as antique white with a strong contrasting color in the moldings, or an offbeat color. In any case, be sure the color harmonizes with the background colors in the rooms adjacent to it. Walls painted a receding color, such as misty-blue, willow-green, or pale aqua, together with either smooth-surface flooring or carpet in a matching color, will make a small foyer look larger.

Informal Halls

If you live informally, you will want simple furniture for your foyer or large hall, with a feeling of warmth and friendliness expressed in the design and color scheme of floors, walls and accessories.

A pleasant provincial feeling may be achieved by using wall-paper with a gay floral chintzlike design or with a small evenly spaced calicolike pattern. You might paint the walls a bright color, or use white to simulate whitewash and add bright contrasting moldings. The floors might be random wood planks, brick flagstone, or a smooth-surface flooring with a spatter-dash effect. Sizable hooked or braided rugs are good informal floor coverings as are colorful textured carpets.

▶

The hall is an ideal place for an architectural wallpaper, but the scale must be right for the area it occupies. In this hall a graceful curving stairway is enhanced by wallpaper of old architectural ruins in correct proportion.

To give a modern hall a warm, informal feeling, you might use a polished cork flooring or a flecked smooth-surface flooring with perhaps bright contemporary rugs or a tweed-effect wall-to-wall carpet.

Stairs, Stair Wells, and Landings

If the stair well opens into the foyer or hall, it is best to carpet the stairs. You can use runners, leaving an area of exposed wood on both sides, or cover them completely. Carpeting on the stairs makes them more attractive, safer, and cuts down noise. For a formal effect, your best choice would be a solid color in a cut-pile, looped-pile, or a slightly textured surface. For an informal feeling, you could use a tone-on-tone, a multicolored looped- or cut-pile tweed-effect carpeting, braided runners, or a gay provincial design. For a unified effect, use the same carpet in the foyer up the stairs to the bedrooms.

◀

This inviting traditional hall is a pleasant preview of other rooms to come. The scenic paper of old New England extends walls and gives the room great distinction; oriental rug adds an elegant note.

▲ *Textured carpeting cuts down noise and unifies this hall and stairway. Coral accent on stool adds a bright note to an otherwise monotone color scheme of beige.*

93

▲ *A wall composed of panels of frosted glass separates the kitchen from entry to this modern apartment, creating a distinctive dining-foyer area.*

94

▲ *Two important pieces of furniture, pictures, and a few sizable accessories are all that are needed to complete the decoration in a small foyer.*

Pale wood doors with attractive molding and handsome brass hardware add a distinctive note to this traditional hall. ▶

The walls of the stair well should tie the lower and upper halls together. If the walls of the foyer or hall are painted, the same color should be used on the stair-well walls. If the walls seem cold and barren, you might hang groupings of gay prints or pictures. Scenic papers add interest to large walls in stair wells.

Stair landings, even those in the new split-level houses, have more personality if they are furnished with one or two pieces of furniture such as a bench or two stools, and with a few important accessories. The accessories might be masses of greens, two or three important pictures, or a grouping of small prints (see illustration, page 97).

Hall Closets

Because the hall closet is mainly used for coats, the decoration of it is often neglected. But bear in mind that in most houses it can be seen from the hall when you open the door. To make it attractive, tie the color scheme in with the hall. You might, for example use a bright contrasting color or a small allover wallpaper design that picks up the colors in the hall.

If you have two hall closets, you're in luck! One could be reserved for coats and the other as a storage space for games and odds and ends. Or the second closet might be turned into a tiny powder room or downstairs lavatory with a small shelf that serves as a dressing table. Since no one will be in it very long, don't be afraid to make it as giddy and gay as you like. Novelty wallpapers, such as a pattern with nostalgic items or a gaily patterned design of bright flowers or fluttering butterflies (hung on both ceiling and walls), will make this tiny room amusing and attractive. If the ceiling is not papered, it can be painted a bright contrasting color. Towels and other accessories can carry out the color scheme effectively if their colors are picked from the wallpaper design.

What About Hallways?

Hallways between various rooms in the house are usually a clutter of doors and broken-up wall spaces. Often they are merely blank, uninteresting corridors, with no special thought given to their decoration.

▶

An attractive solution to the hallway in this split-level house is an arrangement of furniture and important accessories on two levels.

If you have any passageways of this kind, you might try painting the walls a light color, like white, with contrasting moldings. Or paint the ceiling a contrasting color and hang a gallery of prints or pictures on the walls. This kind of treatment will make these passageways so attractive and interesting that you won't notice the broken-up wall spaces. Another simple but effective solution for the hallway problem is to cover the walls with a small allover wallpaper design, such as a tone-on-tone geometric pattern or small calico design, or a simulated textured effect. Small allover designs are easy to hang because repeats are easy to match.

You should leave the floors bare only if you are sure that the noise of footsteps doesn't disturb members of your family when they are sleeping. Wall-to-wall carpet, a runner, or sizable rugs will keep noise at a minimum and make your passageways less dangerous.

Floors and Floor Coverings

Floors play an important part in halls, not only because of the traffic involved, but also because more floor space shows than in rooms where there is more furniture. The type of floor treatment you use should therefore stand hard wear, be easy to clean, and it should be attractive. Also, the kind of hard flooring or floor covering you choose depends on the character you want in your hall. For example, a beautiful parquet floor or a handsome tile effect has

Simple architectural details such as opaque glass panels in entry, wood pillars, and interesting overhead recessed lighting give this modern hall importance.

The small allover wallpaper pattern extending up the stairs, the collection of charming countrified furniture, and polished floor covered with a hand-woven runner give this hall a pleasant nostalgic air.

a formal appearance, while polished cork, brick, slate, or flagstone is informal in feeling. The same consideration of style should determine your choice of rugs or wall-to-wall carpeting. A hooked rug, a simple contemporary design, or a tweedlike carpeting is less formal than a solid-colored carved rug or a dense clipping pile carpeting in a solid color.

Lighting

Lighting in your hall and stairs must be adequate for comfort, yet unobtrusive enough to be beautiful. You might use ceiling fixtures—either traditional or modern in design—but avoid commonplace, stereotyped ceiling fixtures. Even an inexpensive Japanese white paper lantern can give a small contemporary hall more charm than the usual flat ceiling fixture with a round or oblong translucent glass shield.

If you have a console-type table or a chest, wall brackets placed on either side, a lamp placed at either end, or even one large lamp can be used to light a fairly small hall more pleasantly than a ceiling fixture. Even if you have a ceiling fixture that gives adequate light, a lamp on a table or a chest may give your hall a more friendly feeling at nighttime.

Accessories

Above all, accessories for the entrance hall should be distinctive. Harmony with the style of the other furnishings is only one consideration, for accessories should also reflect your own taste and interests. A hall is a good place to display some of your best paintings, or a collection of glass, ceramics, pewter, weather vanes, or whatever you prefer. It's best to group these items and give them special lighting.

If you have only one chest or console table in your foyer, don't put many small fragile objects on it because people will set handbags, gloves, and other things on it, and your treasures may be broken. Even though you may already have a lamp or pair of lamps on the table or chest, a bowl of flowers or leaves or a potted plant makes a pleasing and appropriate additional accessory for your hall.

◀

Here an air of elegance is achieved in the foyer by the use of pale walls and flooring, graceful period pieces, and a few important accessories.

A striking scenic paper of a lovely formal garden gives an illusion of greater space in this foyer. Skillful use of period pieces and unusual accessories add charm.

▶

▲
This inviting kitchen, with pine paneling and cheery color in counter tops and ruffled valances, makes a pleasant place for cooking, breakfasts, and informal meals. Eye-level oven is built into corner.

▶

A drop-leaf table, placed under the windows on the opposite wall of this kitchen, makes a friendly place to eat breakfasts and snacks. Curtains, hung on lower half of the windows, give privacy.

6 Kitchens

Although the kitchen is primarily a place to prepare meals, at the same time it should be an attractive and pleasant place to work.

Even if you can't install new fixtures, you can make your kitchen one of the most attractive rooms in your home by means as simple as introducing a new color scheme. Just covering the ceiling with a gay wallpaper, papering one wall in the dinette with a quaint scenic design or a bold pattern, or covering the floor with an attractive smooth-surface flooring in a bright color will do much to give your kitchen charm. An old kitchen that has an eye-catching color scheme or a few bright touches can have great warmth and interest, and one in which these considerations are neglected, even with the newest equipment, may seem cold and clinical.

If breakfast and lunches are served in your kitchen, interesting old furniture or a new unpainted set enamelled a bright color will give it more personality than stereotyped tables and chairs. If your requirements are for only enough furniture to serve meals to children, a counter or a shelf with brightly colored stools would be sufficient, and the space you save may be useful, especially if your kitchen is small.

If you are planning to remodel an old kitchen, don't think you can solve your problems simply by swapping old fixtures for new ones; it takes careful planning to transform an ugly and badly equipped kitchen into an attractive and efficient one. If you study the illustrations in this chapter you may find, if not a complete kitchen plan that appeals to you, a floor plan in one illustration and an idea for the decoration in another. If you feel that you need outside assistance, put your remodeling job in the hands of either a competent kitchen contractor or a kitchen service. Or, a representative from a cabinet or appliance manufacturer will help you plan your kitchen. Most important, lift your kitchen out of the ordinary with an engaging color scheme or with such decorative touches as colorful cannisters, unusual lighting fixtures, copper molds and pans hung on the wall, or potted plants.

Color Schemes

Since you spend a great deal of time in the kitchen, an attractive scheme using your favorite colors is much more satisfying than an all-white kitchen. You can choose any colors you like, but a light color (not necessarily stark white) for the ceiling will reflect the light better than a dark one.

In choosing a color scheme, incorporate the colors you already have in your kitchen such as colored fixtures and smooth-surfaced flooring. Supposing, for example, that you have dark green flooring and white kitchen equipment, and you would like light turquoise walls with a bright accent color. If you like bold, contrasting colors, you might add a bright flame accent color in such small areas as cannisters, patterned curtains, and chair pads in the dining area. Or if you prefer a more subtle effect, you might paint the ceiling a light citron-yellow and repeat the same color in smaller areas.

Very few kitchens are perfectly constructed. Some are too small, others too narrow or too dark. The right color scheme can make your kitchen cheerful or calm, as you prefer.

To perform specific jobs, there are a few tried and proven fool-the-eye tricks. For example, a cool, light color like aqua or light green will make a small kitchen seem larger. If your room has a southern exposure and gets lots of sunlight, blues, greens, or blue-greens will make it cool and restful. If a northern exposure makes your kitchen dark, such warm colors as yellow, pink, or beige will give it warmth and help to counteract the cold north light. If your kitchen happens to be an old-fashioned barnlike room, consider a dark color for the walls with a matching or contrasting trim to make it look smaller and more friendly. To modify the elongated appearance of a narrow kitchen, you might paint the end walls a darker color than the side walls. To pep up a really gloomy kitchen, try a light, bright background with strong accent colors.

If you give your kitchen a particular theme or mood, build your color scheme around it and add decorative touches that will help to carry out the atmosphere. For example, a country feeling can be

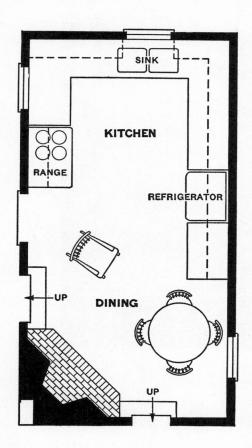

◄

The dining area in this big kitchen, with table and chairs placed in front of platform fireplace and the friendly touch of the Boston rocker, is among the coziest places in the house.

▼

The floor plan of the big dining-kitchen, lower left, shows the cooking end with efficient U-shaped arrangement of equipment and cabinets and the dining end with fireplace built into the corner. The compact cooking end, shown lower right, has a wealth of cabinets. The neat, allover patterned wallpaper combined with pine paneling and hanging ceiling light, reminiscent of the old oil lamp, and braided rug in front of the fireplace, echo the early-American theme.

SINK

KITCHEN

RANGE

REFRIGERATOR

UP

DINING

UP

▲ *Open shelves above the stove to house earthenware and glass, and hanging pots below framed with a shaped wood valance, as well as niches with decorative arrangements of objects, add a distinctive note to this kitchen.*

► *This friendly traditional kitchen is arranged for eating in front of the raised fireplace. Copper pots and colorful plates give the fireplace an individual touch.*

achieved easily by using a gay, bold color scheme and interesting decorative touches. You might paint three walls and the ceiling in a light, clear yellow and cover the remaining wall in simulated white brick or whitewashed wood. You might use a spatter-dash smooth-surface flooring with flecks of red, white, and yellow on a black background. The bright red accent color could be repeated in plaid seat pads and curtains, in pots of geraniums, and in opaque glass shades on an old-fashioned brass hanging lamp over the table. Copper molds and pans grouped on the walls would complete the country theme.

A workable kitchen is built around appliances and storage cabinets. If you are planning to buy new equipment, one of the most important questions you must ask yourself is: "Do I want colored appliances and colored cabinets?" Remember, you must live with your choice for many years. The answer is "yes" if you are completely confident about a particular color scheme, or are sure that the color of the fixtures will harmonize with any changes you might make later on. On the other hand, if you tend to tire of a color or feel unsure about the color scheme you have chosen, stick to white. An almost endless number of attractive color schemes can be worked around white appliances and cabinets. However, yellow, light turquoise, and green also lend themselves to kitchen appliances and cabinets because they harmonize with so many of the colors frequently used in such smaller objects as cooking utensils and other light kitchen equipment.

◄ *A built-in desk unit in this kitchen, lighted by* ▲ *A crisp, neatly-spaced design in wallpaper and*
shielded lighting at top of wall, has ample space on *matching curtains, repeated on table top in a larger*
counter top for typewriter and other items and large *scale, adds sparkle and interest to this uncluttered,*
file drawers below. *space-saving kitchen.*

▲

A wide counter with drawers below, built in under cabinets in this modern kitchen, provides space at one end for shelves to hold cookbooks and radio with telephone nearby. The counter is long enough to seat four people for breakfast. Shielded fluorescent tubes shed a pleasant light.

▲

A pass-through opening with a wide counter, in this small kitchen, makes a convenient place for breakfasts, snacks, and buffet suppers. The opening can be closed with a folding screen. An attractive arrangement of plates, figurines, and glass bottles on graduated shelves in the kitchen adds an individual note.

▲

Notice how this Pullman kitchen looks just as at-tractive when the doors are open as when they are closed. Papered with an amusing wallpaper, with utensils hung on metal racks, the interior becomes a pleasant prospect.

◀

Here the problem of a Pullman kitchen opening directly into a small foyer was solved by making the doors a part of the decorative scheme. The doors are painted to match the walls with a lighter shade in the moldings and handles. Flooring laid in squares gives foyer distinction.

111

Walls

Today, there is a host of relatively new easy-to-apply wall covering products which can transform a dingy kitchen into a sparkling gem. There are easy-to-apply washable paints, scrubbable wallpapers (some are prepasted and trimmed), and washable wall coverings such as plastic tiles, Sanitas and Wall-Tex. Then, of course there are more expensive materials such as wood and ceramic tiles. Wood walls, however, should be properly finished because otherwise they absorb stains and soil, while ceramic tiles offer the same advantages for a kitchen as for a bathroom.

There are many attractive ways of giving your kitchen a new look. Painting the walls a lovely color with a light-colored contrasting ceiling is one simple way of changing the entire appearance of your kitchen. Or, if you want an unusual effect, you might cover the ceiling with a gaily patterned nondirectional scrubbable wallpaper. Yet another alternative, if you feel that the dinette or dining area looks cramped or needs a lift, you might cover one wall with a gay scenic paper or with a bold pattern. Or, you can give a kitchen with painted walls and ceiling new interest by using a colorful print at the windows and on chair pads; be sure that the print picks up the color in the walls and adds a bright accent color.

▲ *This colorful kitchen stands at the right of the entry hall, opens into dining area for easy serving. Counter bar provides convenient space for breakfast and snacks.*

112

▲ *A counter extending from sink area, along one wall, gives ample room for work as well as for meals. Colorful chintz curtains and potted geraniums add bright notes in the kitchen.*

▼ *The easy, livable plan of this kitchen area provides for informal meals or buffet serving and a compact work area. Panel illumination in ceiling keeps area well lighted.*

This kitchen bears the stamp of personal planning. Keyed to the individual living pattern of the family, an island with a wide counter top splits the kitchen and the family-TV area. Distinctive touches, such as the quaint wallpaper, striped café curtains, and hanging brass lamp, help to carry out the countrified feeling in the family room. This easy, livable plan creates an atmosphere for shared family activities or for informal entertaining.

114

▼ *Brown Formica walls and ceiling act as a foil for color scheme of light turquoise and muted coral in this modern kitchen. Beyond the cook-and-serve center is a large bank of storage cabinets to house dinnerware and glassware, along with quantities of canned and packaged goods. It is made of wall cabinets in standard sizes, hung right down to the floor. Pegboard and counter, at entry to kitchen, help keep tab on family business.*

▲ *There's ample space around the sink of the kitchen shown above to collect dishes for the dishwasher at right of sink. The rounded counter top provides plenty of space for informal meals, or for stacking dishes, or for rolling piecrusts or cooling cookies. Notice the relationship of refrigerator freezer to cook-and-serve center.*

▶

This laundry center, at entire end of kitchen, includes matching washer and dryer, storage for supplies, and tilting bin for soiled dish towels.

◀

The compact cooking area, installed in front of the windows in this kitchen, makes cooking a pleasure. Range top has work space on either side with storage space below. Wall oven installed in unit at one side has storage above and below.

▶

The island counter in this modern kitchen makes a convenient place to stack dishes, or for informal meals, or as an extra work space. Built-in shelves, at one end of counter, house small electrical appliances, radio, bread box, and other things needed for kitchen.

▲ *This attractive kitchen with dining area for informal meals is as inviting as it is practical. The built-in island with shelves and storage cupboard, on the dining area side, acts as a serving counter and divider for range installed on the kitchen side. The gay plaid wallpaper unifies the kitchen and dining areas. Wood-grained cabinets go well with everything from painted dining chairs to matchstick blinds and plaid wallpaper.*

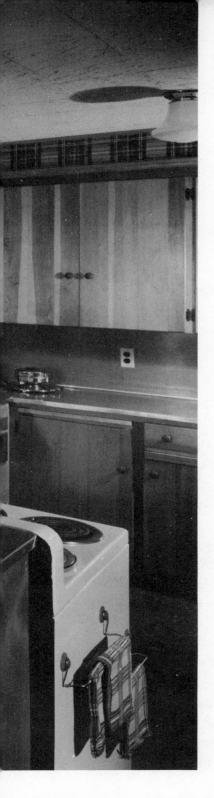

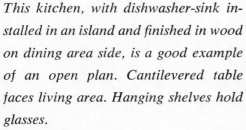

The personal touches in this countrified kitchen, such as painted motifs, trivet handles on pine cabinets, and growing plants on window wall, make creative cooking a pleasure.

This kitchen, with dishwasher-sink installed in an island and finished in wood on dining area side, is a good example of an open plan. Cantilevered table faces living area. Hanging shelves hold glasses.

Floors

A kitchen floor must be able to take hard wear for many years, so be sure to choose a flooring that can be easily cleaned and that won't show scuff marks, stains, or soil. If your kitchen gets lots of traffic, a dark color with a marbleized, strié, or mottled design will show soil and marks less than a light color. But remember, the color and pattern must harmonize with the other colors and the style of decoration in the kitchen. For example, a spatter-dash smooth-surface flooring makes a charming background for a provincial kitchen with knotty pine cabinets and a wallpaper with a quaint documentary design, while marbleized-, strié-, or terrazzo-effect flooring blends pleasantly with a modern kitchen.

Though nothing is more charming than ceramic tile or waxed brick, you'll find that such smooth-surface floorings as vinyl, rubber tile, or asphalt tile are easier to walk on.

Furniture

You must have at least one stool or chair in the kitchen (for certain tasks can or should be performed sitting down), and most kitchens also have a table and chairs or a counter bar for eating. If you have a counter-bar arrangement, stools are most practical and can double for general kitchen use.

Even though a kitchen must be practical, you can use an attractive table and chairs in the dining area. For example, a round early American table with painted Hitchcock chairs would add an individual touch to a kitchen with a provincial look; or woven reed chairs with iron legs and a round metal table with an opaque glass top would add a warm charming note to a modern kitchen.

One piece of kitchen furniture that can be most useful is a cart-on-wheels; the best type is one that has drop leaves and a washable, stain-resistant top. You'll find many uses for a cart-on-wheels. Not only can it be used for service in the dining room, living room, porch, and terrace, but it can also provide extra counter space in the kitchen, especially for taking food out of the refrigerator or a wall oven.

Lighting

More than any other room in your home, the kitchen needs a bright light to make the work you do in this room easier and more pleasant. The ideal lighting is a combination of good general illumination and enough specific lighting in certain areas to eliminate shadows.

In this remodeled kitchen, with large curved top opening into dining area, the wood-grained cabinets blend pleasantly with wallpaper in dining area and ceiling in kitchen, and with finely scaled wrought-iron chairs and glass-topped table in dining area.

Inventive ideas on space-planning and storage are incorporated in this kitchen. The sink, counter space, and storage are installed under corner windows. Extra storage cabinets are hung on wall space above windows and on either side.

A simple close-to-the-ceiling fixture, centered in the area, will give your kitchen the best and the most cheerful allover illumination.

To obtain the best results, you should have specific lighting over such areas as the kitchen range, the work counter, the sink, and the dining area. As a rule, work areas should be lighted by fluorescent fixtures which may be painted to match the cabinets to which they are attached. Warm, white, de luxe fluorescent tubes not only blend well with incandescent light, but also complement food and colors. It is important to choose a good color in fluorescent tubes; a wrong choice here may result in bilious, unattractive lighting.

The lighting for the dining area can be almost any kind of down light that harmonizes with your decorative theme. For example, if the over-all theme in your kitchen is modern, the dining area might be lighted with a pulley lamp hung on the ceiling or wall, with a cluster of contemporary down lights, or with any other attractive contemporary fixture that gives a good directed light. On the other hand, if your kitchen is provincial in feeling, an old hanging brass lamp or a country-type chandelier will give your dining area charm and individuality as well as good light.

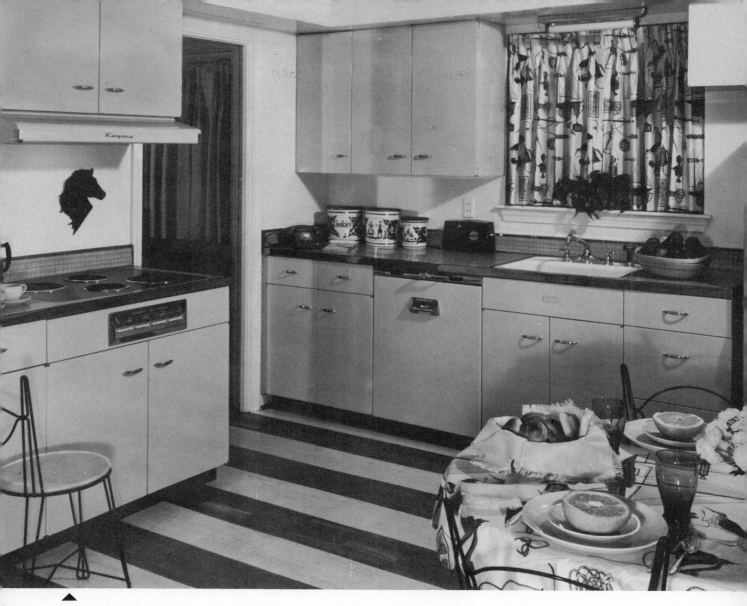

The color scheme of citron yellow, charcoal, and white, with turquoise accents, used in a dramatic posterlike way, gives this modern kitchen great distinction. The predominating color, citron yellow, is repeated in cabinets and equipment. Alternating stripes of charcoal and white flooring have an effect of widening the floor area. Turquoise accents in gay chintz curtains, table cloth, and glassware add decorative interest.

The kitchen opposite is as inviting to work in as it is to look at. The warmth of the knotty pine walls, with scalloped cornice and early American hinges on cupboards, gives it an old-fashioned cozy look.

▲ *An interesting use of wood, brick, and wallpaper,*
along with such decorative touches as turned posts,
unusual lighting, and scalloped copper hood on
range, supply a pleasant informal background that
makes cooking, eating, and entertaining a pleasure
in this combination dining-living-room-kitchen.

124

▼ *Now you can buy a packaged kitchen of cabinet-and-appliance ensembles that can be moved into place with a minimum of installation. The appliances blend to give the much-wanted built-in look, as shown in this kitchen.*

◀ *Two window walls in this dining area look out onto a garden. The dining area and kitchen are separated by a built-in room divider, rising above eye level, with storage unit below and opening above that allows air to circulate.*

125

Accessories

Most accessories for the kitchen are useful articles, but many of them are decorative as well.

If you want to decorate the walls of your kitchen, don't overlook such useful items as colorful cooking utensils, copper molds and pans, and attractive spice cabinets. Pictures and old prints also add a charming decorative note to kitchen walls.

You can make an open cupboard a focal point by arranging such useful articles as tall pepper grinders, handsome cruets, earthenware jars, apothecary jars, or candy jars to hold staples. Then, of course, every kitchen should have an electric clock and a radio. The clock can be one of the intriguing new modern designs, or such a traditional timepiece as an old, round, painted tole clock. And you can find portable radios in almost any color to blend with your color scheme. Potted plants add a bright, friendly touch to a kitchen, as do baskets holding colorful fruit and vegetable arrangements.

▲ *This kitchen is built around automatic appliances. Sliding-door cabinets above appliances hold often-used items. Doors can be removed for cleaning inside. Metal strip above shields lights.*

▲ *In this carefree kitchen is a delightfully comfortable corner for mixing and serving, and outlets are at hand for small appliances. Notice lazy susan for easy storage of canned goods and intercom set built into corner.*

▶

In the same kitchen the sink (with disposer and one-hand lever faucet control) and counter join smoothly. The dishwasher is a full 6 inches wider than usual and holds service for eight.

▲

This cheerful family room has a mixture of woven rattan and wrought-iron furniture. The sofas are composed of two wooden frames with foam rubber mattresses and wedge bolsters. The wallpaper with playing card motifs makes a striking one-wall decoration. Bold squares of asphalt tile dramatize floor.

128

7 Family Rooms and Studies

Because the living room in today's small house does not adequately accommodate various members of the family who are trying simultaneously to converse, read the papers, watch television, or just relax, a need has been created for some area apart from the living room for relaxation and a change of scenery. If this is your problem, expense permitting, a separate recreation room (or a second casual family room) is the best solution. Such a room saves wear and tear on the living room and provides space for a variety of family activities and hobbies. It is ideal for entertaining large groups at buffet suppers, club luncheons, and children's parties, and makes an excellent place for teenagers to entertain their friends, or for the children to play on rainy days. The essential requirements for a family room are comfort, cheerful surroundings, and ample space for large groups of people.

Since the family room is primarily a place for relaxation, all furnishings should be simple, comfortable, flexible, and easy to maintain. The furniture should be sturdy but light enough to be moved about and rearranged easily. The flooring should be of a material that wears well and cleans easily, such as smooth-surface flooring, slate, or concrete. Fabrics should be durable and washable.

Whether your family room is in the basement, the attic, or an added wing, it's a good idea to install a snack bar or kitchenette, possibly in a closet, with a counter bar opening into the room. Ideally it should have adequate equipment, including running water, a small refrigerator, a cooking arrangement, and storage space for dishes, glasses, and kitchen utensils.

You may even want a barbecue, either the kind that can be installed in a fireplace or one of the portable charcoal cooking units on wheels that can be rolled out of sight when the cooking is finished.

Color Schemes

One of the prime requisites for a recreation or family room is a gay, cheerful color scheme. However, this doesn't mean that the colors should be garish. When planning your color scheme, bear in mind that the colors must be a background for relaxed living, yet give a lift to tired spirits. Here are some color ideas that may be helpful.

If your family room has very little daylight or is a north room, a predominantly yellow color scheme will give it feeling of sunlight and warmth. It might be a color scheme of either light tints and darker shades of yellow (monochromatic) or yellowish colors that are adjacent to each other, such as citron-yellow, daffodil-yellow, and mustard analogous) with a sparkling accent color, such as turquoise or blue. Provincial furniture in mellow woods, or rattan, woven reed, and wrought-iron go well with yellow rooms.

If your recreation area is a dark, cheerless room, pink or red as the dominant color will give it a warm, stimulating atmosphere that should appeal to your family and friends. For a fresh, light-hearted atmosphere, try pinks in various tints with white as a foil. This type of room makes a wonderful background for graceful, painted— wrought-iron furniture (see illustration, page 141).

If you like provincial, rustic furniture and you want to create a country atmosphere, a muted red, like the color of old bricks, makes an excellent background for mellow woods, but it must be accented with a contrasting color such as blue or green. If so much muted red disturbs you, neutralize it with beige tones in upholstery and draperies.

If your family room has contemporary iron or rattan furniture, use lots of flame or cherry-red contrasted with white, and perhaps green or blue as an accent color.

In a family room that has plenty of light or a southern exposure, a color scheme with a dominant green or blue might appeal to you. In order to make these cool colors gay and cheerful, you must use a warm contrasting color; red, orange, or yellow would add the necessary brightness.

▲

Contemporary study-guest room shows ceiling-high bookshelves with built-in cupboards and window-width desk below. Handsome, practical rubber-tile floor blends with period chairs, patterned ceiling paper, day bed with boxed pillows to look like a modern sofa.

A rather small study-library takes on stature with built-in storage space, combining window seat, high-up bookshelves, commodious corner desk. Quiet related colors of woodwork, curtains, and room-size rug add their quota of easy space. Spicy paprika accents the cushions, chair, ceiling lamp.

▶

Furniture and Furniture Arrangement

Your family room can be decorated any way you like as long as it is simple and cheerful. Whatever you do, don't fill the room with a depressing assortment of old hand-me-downs or with heavy, bulky pieces of furniture, such as enormous sofas, bulky chairs, and heavy tables. There is a wide variety of light-weight furniture available that is just as durable as heavy, bulky furniture. And remember that proper proportion is just as important in a casual family room as in any other room in your home.

Your family room can be gay and bright with simple modern styles, pretty and light with graceful outdoor-indoor wrought-iron pieces, or distinctly provincial with mellow wood furniture; it can be dramatized in any way that suits your fancy.

Because the function of a family room is to accomodate varied activities, there should be one or more tables for cards and other table games. It's a good idea to choose light-weight but sturdy tables that can be put together to form one long table for sit-down or buffet dining or as a long hobby table. Chairs, too, should be light-weight and adaptable to many purposes, such as dining and games; they might double as extra seating in the living room.

Even if you must use hand-me-downs, wood pieces that are light and simple can be refinished, and the sofa and lounge chairs can be slipcovered. Be sure to consider the scale and proportion of each piece, as well as the flexibility of the styles for rearrangements and dual-purpose use. If the sofa and lounge chairs, for example, are old-fashioned bulky pieces with sagging springs, your best bet is to sell them or give them away. You can substitute relatively inexpensive pieces, such as a couch with a webbed wooden frame and a slipcovered foam rubber mattress, and light-weight chairs. The chairs may be molded plastic, metal, or rattan armchairs with slipcovered seat and back cushions, or even the familiar folding director's chairs, with canvas seat and back.

A television set and a record player are almost essential. These facilities enable you to hold impromptu dances and informal TV suppers, and provide invaluable entertainment for family gatherings.

Fabrics

Since your family room will get lots of hard wear, you should make it easy to maintain. Choose colorful, washable, preshrunk, and if possible, crease-resistant fabrics for slipcovers, cushion covers, draperies, and curtains. Denim, sailcloth, ticking, permanent-finish chintz, cretonne, cotton rep, and cotton gabardine make sturdy slipcovers or cushion covers. These materials are firmly woven and have

132

▲ *A spacious family room with dining facilities invites a variety of activities unimpeded by scattered furniture. One wall provides shelves for accessories and books, cupboards, hi-fi radio-and-speaker. Built-in bench has storage space and seats four.*

a smooth surface; most of them are colorfast, washable, and shrink-proof. Since many of these fabrics hang in soft folds, they can be used effectively for draperies. Many translucent fabrics, referred to as *casement cloth*, are excellent for windows in family rooms because they can be drawn to exclude glaring sunlight and to ensure privacy. Casement cloth is made in a variety of weaves and fibers, including many synthetic fibers, such as nylon, orlon, dacron, Fiberglas, and Fortisan. Most of these casement cloths wash easily, are soil-resistant, and require little pressing.

Equally important, of course, is your choice of colors harmonious with the over-all scheme in your family room. One simple rule for fabrics is to choose solid colors if you have a pattern in your walls or floor. But if your walls and floor have solid colors, an important pattern for major fabric areas, with one or two touches in solid colors, will give the room interest and importance. Or you can use only solid-colored fabrics with one color predominating.

Split bamboo or wood shades are practical and suitable for windows in a family room, as are shutters. Many of the shades, with woven bands of color, need neither draperies nor curtains.

▲ *A study-guest room, 9 by 13 feet, captures space by built-in bookshelves, bed and cupboard, as well as sewing corner. Soft wood-tone paneling, light blue ceiling, and wall-to-wall carpet complete the illusion.*

Sewing room-within-a-room is built-in at corner with effect of drawer-front storage unit. Chair pulls out and in flush. Sewing machine drops beneath counter top when not in use. ▶

◀ *In a small house, built-ins save space in the guest and family room combined. A radio-phonograph unit at end of built-in couch-bed shares a corner with neat small desk.*

An inviting family room has an end wall that combines a stunning raised hearth, copper-hooded fireplace, bookshelves, and TV. Sliding glass doors on patio can be completely covered up. There is a piano in the room and a floor to dance on.

Pecky cypress wall dramatizes one end of family room designed for entertaining. Ample built-in sofa turns a corner with shelf table for snacks.

Walls

Wall treatment in a family room should be keyed to the decorative theme. For example, a knotty-pine wall—whether real wood or simulated—and sturdy provincial furniture would give a family room a casual, country atmosphere. On the other hand, a fresh, gay outdoor atmosphere could be achieved by using a scenic paper with an outdoor design on one wall and white simulated brick on the other three; here light, contemporary, wrought-iron furniture would carry out your theme.

Floors

Floors can be as varied as you like, but it is wise to choose a flooring of a resilient, washable, and easy-to-care-for material such as asphalt, vinyl, or rubber tile, since this floor will get a lot of hard wear. Also, smooth-surface flooring is desirable because it is best for dancing or for playing group games.

▲ *Study and family room combine for ease in a space for varied activity. Built into the recesses at each side of the white-painted brick fireplace are the record player and the TV set. Upholstery is sturdy, and the floor easy to care for.*

◀ *A study snug as a ship's cabin picks up space with wall-to-wall carpet, tone-on-tone ceiling and walls. Ceiling-high bookshelves and built-in desk add to trim ship-shape feeling. A sea-lover reads here in peace.*

139

A family room with a five-way wall—
bookshelves, Formica ledge for easy
buffets, television, left below; at right,
cabinet for glasses and supplies and, at
center, radio, phonograph, and storage
for records.

If the wall treatment is an important feature in your room, the
flooring should be unobtrusive. It may be marbleized, a spatter-dash
or strié effect, or a solid color.

If you want rugs, either to add warmth and color to your flooring,
or to pull together a furniture grouping—a fireplace group, for
instance—consider accent or area rugs. For walls with a scenic pattern
or a paper with a bold design, use rugs in a solid color or a tweedlike texture to avoid competing with the walls. But if your walls and
floors are generally plain, you can use patterned rugs. Small rugs
are easy to roll up—an advantage you will appreciate if you are
entertaining a large group for a buffet supper or if the teenagers have
an impromptu dance.

Lighting

Lighting is especially important if your family room is in a dark
basement. For general illumination, recessed down-lighting will disguise the fact that you are in a basement, but it is fairly expensive.
To give the illusion of daylight and for general illumination you
may need to light only certain areas; a concealed light over a long
wall or concealed lighting in small window niches in a cellar might be

▲ *Pretty, practical pink-and-white basement family room, with a penthouse air. Walls are of combed white shingle, floors of sturdy vinyl. Wrought-iron furniture includes table for games or refreshments. Louvered shutters extend to floor below high windows.*

A downstairs family room dedicated to fun and games features a decorative shuffleboard pattern inlaid in the asphalt tile floor. Comfort and color are keyed high throughout. Pine-paneled wall boasts counter for easy buffets.

▲ *A convivial basement family room is easy to maintain with its marbelized vinyl floor, knotty pine paneling extending up to a high shelf, sturdy iron, wood, and rattan pieces. Gay rug defines the conversation center.*

In this all-purpose family room, there's a cozy place in front of the fireplace for conversation and dining. Also there's a counter along one wall for buffet service and a convenient table for playing cards.

145

sufficient. Specific lighting for game tables, ping-pong table, and snack bar should be down-lighting. A hanging light (either stationary or the pulley type) is best for these areas. Other specific lighting, say for a conversation grouping around a fireplace, might be portable —such as sturdy table or floor lamps—or wall pulley lamps. Lamps add warmth and intimacy to a family room.

Family Rooms and Studies

Each of the illustrations in this chapter demonstrates how a recreation room can be used to great advantage. These pictures also show how wallpaper, paint, floor coverings, fabrics, and furniture can make your family room as attractive as any other room in the house.

The Library or Study

Although a library or study, in the strictest sense, is intended primarily for reading and study, the old-fashioned library with book-shelves from floor to ceiling and conventional library furniture is almost extinct.

In the average small house today, the study is usually a fairly small room that must also serve as a guest bedroom. Accordingly, it must be decorated in an entirely different manner from the old-fashioned library. This type of small room, closed off from the rest of the house, is an ideal solution to the problem of quiet. Here the occupant can retire and take a nap, go over business accounts, write letters, or just relax and read. It may also serve as a retreat for father and mother when the younger members of the family are entertaining in the living room. Or, the room may be used for an overflow of guests who want to play bridge or discuss business, while the other guests are in the living room. The study also makes a congenial place for after-dinner coffee and conversation, especially if you are having a small dinner party.

Essential requirements for today's study or den are comfort, coziness, and cheerful surroundings. It should have enough windows to provide ample daylight for those who use it during the day, and a warm pleasant atmosphere at night.

Furniture for the Study

Since the study may often serve as a guest room, where comfort is a prime requisite, careful planning is essential. First of all, you

Basement room with rather formal air is also relaxed and comfortable; low armless chairs, round table, zebra rug spell ease and quiet charm.

Traditional and countrified is this basement family room, with its beam and rough plaster, early-American chairs, pine panels, and chintz.

▲ *Trading Post—Post Office décor for this basement family room points to teenage members who will love "No Credit" sign on cash register set on snack bar. Light knotty-pine walls and mural add space.*

need a double-purpose bed that may be used as a sofa by day, yet provide sleeping accommodations at night. You can use a simple daybed, composed of a box-mattress and springs on legs, with boxed pillows or bolsters across the back to give it the appearance and comfort of a sofa. You can also find a wide selection of sofa-beds, or even small chair-beds (if you're really pushed for space). Since the average study is small and a double sofa-bed leaves little space when it is unfolded at night, you would be wise to use a lighter-scaled single sofa-bed and, if more sleeping room is required, use a fold-up cot in addition. Modern fold-up cots are comfortable and can be stored easily in a small closet.

There should be at least one comfortable armchair, possibly with a matching ottoman or stool which can be used as extra seating. Small stools or floor cushions are also useful adjuncts.

Table space is an absolute necessity; a large table on each side of the couch, or a sizable corner table placed at right angles between two daybeds would be adequate. There should be enough table room to hold a good reading lamp, books, magazines, an ashtray, a container for cigarettes, and other small objects that might be used in this room. If there isn't room for a reading lamp, you can use wall pulley lamps over the table.

▲

Basement room is a gay retreat for the young of the family. Hot pink walls have harlequin murals, drapery is also painted on. Snack bar is covered with striped wallpaper, smooth floor is an invitation to the dance.

▶

Family game room, geared for entertaining large groups, adaptable for cards, dancing, refreshments. In midnight blue and white with bright green accents, it has indirect lighting. Canopy-like draperies conceal unwieldy beams. Chairs are turn-of-century bentwood.

A coffee table or two small tables that can be pushed together also help to make a study more comfortable; they can be used for mixing drinks before dinner, serving coffee after dinner, or (if you are having a large buffet supper) as a cocktail table for overflow guests to use for their plates or trays.

A desk is also a necessity for writing letters or going over household or business accounts. Since the typewriter has become important for everyday writing, it's a good idea to choose a desk that will accommodate a portable typewriter. If the desk is to be used as an office for household accounts or other business, consider one with space for filing, writing paper, and other materials. But remember, if the desk is to be used by guests, it should also be equipped with things a guest may need, such as ink, pen, pencils, envelopes, stamps, scissors, and scotch tape or a jar of paste. A desk must have a good light—either a portable lamp or a wall pulley lamp. If the desk is intended primarily for guests, it can be a writing table that doubles as a dressing table.

Bookshelves and storage space are also an important part of a guest bedroom-study. Hanging bookshelves are often most desirable for they may be arranged to leave the lower part of the wall free for furniture. A simple method of hanging bookshelves is to use punched metal strips and metal brackets to support shelves. The punched metal strips allow for adjustable shelves.

A study should also have storage space to hold such things as records, sewing materials, and odds and ends that can't be stored in other rooms, as well as adequate space for articles your guests will bring with them.

To meet this problem, you can build in storage units, or you can buy separate storage pieces (some may either be lined up horizontally, or stacked vertically). You will find a variety of ready-made storage units in department stores in both modern and traditional designs.

There are also many kinds of special storage pieces; these include: units designed to hold both a man's and a woman's small articles of clothing; combinations of two storage chests with drawers, connected by a center section that forms a writing table or a dressing table; combination bookshelf-storage units with drawers or a cabinet below and shelves—either open or enclosed with doors—above. These compact storage units, whether built-in or ready-made, are space-saving in a small study.

▶

Study cum *music for a music-loving family. A small electric organ fits beneath the bookshelves in a corner of the room. Lyre-back chair, curtains of a soft sheer fabric, printed with musical instruments, strike appropriate notes.*

Often the television set, radio, and record player are placed in the study. However, if these are the only units that you have in your home and the study is to be used a great deal by guests, it would be more practical to install these appliances in the living room or family room and put a small portable television set or radio in the study. If you do install these units in the study, you can save space by enclosing them in a closet or cabinet. Or, they may be arranged on a bench against a wall space below a row of hanging bookshelves.

Color Schemes

Since the study is a cozy, intimate room, it's better to choose soft, muted colors, than the gay, bright ones you might use in a family room. If you choose quiet, closely related colors for the walls, floor, upholstery, and curtains, your small study will seem larger than it is. Books, magazines, pictures, pillows, and other accessories can provide the bright accent colors in the room. For example, you might choose warm beige and mellow wood tones with bright accents of cantaloupe, or a background of cool greens with bright accents of cerulean-blue and citron.

Floors

Wall-to-wall carpeting or a large room-size rug also helps to make a small study look larger and to reduce noise. Two of the relatively inexpensive sturdy carpetings that are easy to maintain and that withstand hard wear are tufted nylon and Acrilan. They are available in cut pile (some with a permanent twist effect) and in interesting tweedlike looped effects. Depending on how you decorate your study, hard flooring, such as vinyl, brick, cork, and wood might also be practical. But polished flooring often gives a room a cold aspect, and noise becomes a problem. A practical solution is a sizable area rug, which will add warmth and color and keep noise at a minimum. Today area rugs are made in sizes suitable for small rooms. A good size for the average small study is either a 4- by 6-foot rug, or a 6- by 9-foot rug. You will find a good selection of relatively inexpensive area rugs in stores, such as solid-colored rugs with interesting textures (some with carved borders and allover carved designs), tweed effects, and simple geometric designs.

▲ *One end of this small study is used for built-ins, with careful attention to architectural detail and furnishing. The television set occupies the center section with shelves and storage on each side. Vertically striped blinds, like those on the cupboard doors, close over the set's screen. Brass ceiling light, leather chair, other treasures lend elegance here.*

▲ *An old-fashioned raised fireplace, with a grouping of sturdy pine furniture, makes a focal point in this family room. A table, placed in front of a window, can be used for games and dining.*

Lighting

Although it is always best to have some kind of general illumination, specific lighting for reading, writing, card playing, and so on, may give enough light for general illumination in a small room.

Accessories

Be sure to save part of your budget for accessories. Although books themselves contribute color, pattern, and interest to a study, you may find that your bookshelves have more individuality and interest if you combine books with a variety of objects. You might use a combination such as a collection (model ships, or shells, or reproductions of ancient sculpture), as well as greens, magazines, and books. Also, the desk is a good place for a grouping of unusual accessories, such as a good-looking lamp, a handsome antique inkwell, an unusual box for pencils or cigarettes, and a colorful paper weight. And consider putting your choicest picture or a grouping of interesting pictures in the study. Don't be afraid to mix periods, as long as the proportions and character of the objects you use are appropriate to your decorative scheme.

Dining bar in a handsome pine-paneled kitchen is a perfect spot for family meals. The deep counter has easy-to-clean plastic top; stools push under it when they're not in use. The back section of counter is used for storing serving trays.

For this family room a cement floor was chosen for durability, ease of upkeep. Scored in checkers, it was painted to pick up wood tones and to contrast pleasantly with stonework.

▲ *For privacy and protection, a terrace room is screened from the street on one side by the house itself, on the other by a louver-like fence, painted white. It makes a pleasing view through glass from the interior.*

8 Outdoor Living

The term *outdoor living* nowadays covers a lot of different things, varying with the section of the country, with the climate, and with the character of the neighborhood—urban, suburban, or really rural. But one thing is sure: people were never so conscious of its importance as they are today.

Outdoor-living areas are planned for as if they were another room in the house (as indeed, in the case of the widely popular semi-enclosed terrace or closed-in porch, they may well become). It's a poor house design that does not take outdoor-living possibilities into consideration, and only a very unknowing builder would fail to place a house on the lot so as to give the owners the maximum of space for the kind of outdoor living people look for and want today.

No matter where you live—from California to Florida to Maine—what you'll want most from your outdoor-living area is a reasonable degree of seclusion and privacy. Gone are the days when "sitting on on the veranda and watching the people go by" was the great national pastime. Outdoor living has taken to the "back yard" the emphasis is on relaxation and family use. And even where the patio or terrace must be close to the street or to a neighbor's boundary line, some sort of screening—a wall, a woven stake fence, or thick shrubbery—is considered an absolute necessity.

So one of the first things you'll want to consider if you are buying or building a new house or remodeling an old one is the logical place for your outdoor-living area and whether it can be sufficiently screened from the street and the neighbors to make it a pleasant place for you and your family.

There are other things to consider too: its relation to the sun—morning or afternoon—and to the prevailing winds; and its location in relation to your indoor rooms. For instance, if your outdoor-living area is likely to be used mostly for adult entertaining or by older members of the family for relaxation, you might like to have it open off the living room or dining room. But if it is to be used a good part of the time as a play area for small children, you'll want to be sure it is visible from your kitchen window.

The planning and furnishing of outdoor-living areas is a new and specialized chapter in decoration. And the open patio or terrace is not the only outdoor-living area included in these special decoration techniques and ideas; they embrace also the old-fashioned screened porch, the glassed-in sun parlor, the covered terrace, the sun deck atop your garage, the breezeway between the garage and your house. Any of these areas may be turned into a delightful "room" for outdoor living.

Consider Your Needs and Requirements

No matter what kind of area you have, begin by jotting down the ways you want to use it, for this will help you work out your plans.

A secluded outdoor living arrangement is shaded by a magnificent tree, a part of the color scheme of reds and greens. Terrace is bounded by high redwood fence.

A small house grows roomy with this wide terrace-lounge added. Gray cement brick makes floor and pierced walls. Bright canvas chairs, masses of colored foliage, and flowers in pots create a garden room.

◀ *A patio becomes a very private outdoor dining room when surrounded by a high stone wall ringed with shady trees. It's equipped with cooking and warming ovens built of stone into the wall. Wrought-iron furniture is light and graceful but strong. Grass-grown paving is edged with shrubbery.*

▼ *Transform carport into terrace with trellis for privacy and smooth flagstone pavement. Roof of the carport's light metal framework is glazed with translucent plastic panes against the rain. Scaled to size is wrought-iron furniture, and coffee table—buffet.*

What kind of family are you? Do you and your husband like to lie on a chaise and read, listen to music, and talk quietly with a few friends? Or do you prefer more gregarious activities with large groups in for cards or buffet suppers? Or does the teenage crowd congregate for games and dancing? For these two latter activities you'll need extra chairs, extra folding equipment, stacks of extra cushions, and a place to store them when not in use. You might ask yourself, too, whether your family is the cook-out, do-it-yourself type, or would rather see alfresco meals roll smoothly out of the kitchen via a wheeled cart? In the latter case, there's not much point in building an elaborate barbecue grill, for it will seldom be used. A simple portable grill will probably be all you will ever need.

Next consider climate conditions in your locality. Do you have a long sunny dry season balanced by a short rainy season (typical of the Southwest), or are showers prevalent, with a certain number of rainy days any time of the year (as on the Eastern seaboard)? In the latter case it is important for you to plan to have some part of your patio under cover, if only to protect your furniture in bad weather.

And while you're on the subject of climate, analyze the quality of your sunshine. Is the midday sun so hot that it "bounces" right off a paved terrace into the windows of the house? In this case, plan your patio so that it will be shaded at noonday by a tree, an angle of the house, an eggcrate trellis, latticed screens, an awning, or some other kind of shelter. Planting grass between the paving blocks of your terrace or breaking up the area with turf or flower beds will also tend to reduce the reflection of heat, and at the same time will add to the charm of your outdoor-living area.

To screen or not to screen is another problem governed by local conditions. Do you live in an area that is blessedly free of insects the year round, both night and day? Or, let's face it, do you need at

▲ *The pleasant luxury of privacy out of doors was achieved here by means of a higher-than-eye-level wall of siding to match the wall of the house. Stone-and-cement floor is edged with lawn and pretty planting. Inexpensive garden furniture in bright colors, durable and weather-resistant, makes a gay and inviting terrace.*

◀

An intimate patio for relaxing, entertaining, living in with sun or shade. Light wrought-iron and rattan furniture, shell seats are easy to move about, store in the house. A trellis, door shutters, and topiary trees are painted on the white of the house for a year-round garden look.

165

least part of the area screened if you are going to get any real enjoyment of it after dark? The new aluminum and plastic screening is light and easy to install and doesn't rust and streak; it can be put up in panels or attached directly to a wooden framework. You can also find on the market a modestly priced prefabricated screened-in "room" which is easy to assemble, and comes complete with awning "roof" and an entrance doorway. It can be set up to stand either against the side of the house or alone.

After you've decided on your personal requirements, you might consider whether your house calls for a casual, informal approach (with redwood chaises, trestle tables, plain folding deck chairs, and so forth) or for more formal treatment (wrought-iron or sleek modern styles).

Your next step will be to make a plot plan of your patio or a floor plan of your porch. This will help you to decide not only exactly what furniture you will need and where, but also where you will need fencing for privacy, where you should plant greenery for shade or additional screening, and where you may need to set up a windbreak. Although you'll want furniture which can be moved about, a plan will help you decide where your dining table and chaises will usually stand and what corner you might screen off for sun bathing.

◀

A shady house in the pines has a sun-washed terrace —a virtual extension of the living room. Louvered doors are flanked by ceiling-to-floor glass windows which bring the outdoors in. Comfortable casual chairs are light, easy to carry in and out.

▲ *This terrace, an extension of the living room, is open to sunshine, but sheltered by the overhang of the roof which offers shady areas. Furniture is low and casual. Planters hold shrubs, flowers.*

Opening off the dining room, a terrace is really an all-purpose outdoor room. It's altogether private for fair-weather dining, entertaining. Latticed roof and walls cast pattern of light and shade. ▶

Background Materials

The kind of paving you choose will be governed to some extent by the style of your house. Flagstones, brick squares, ceramic tiles, or cement blocks can be set directly into the ground with sand or grass between, or into concrete. Cracked marble or granite gravel-edged with bricks or 2- by 4-inch boards makes an interesting terrace floor. In the lumber country, a beautiful paving can be made by cutting a large log crosswise like a loaf of bread and setting the circles of cut wood into the ground with turf growing around them.

You can use various materials for fencing, too. Woven stick fencing, which can be bought ready made, has the advantage of being flexible and easy to install. Woven plywood or different kinds of wood, depending on the function of the fence, are also attractive and practical materials.

What Kind of Furniture?

Let's suppose you've decided to your own satisfaction how your family will use your outdoor-living area. You've marked off on your plan where you want the dining table, the barbecue, and the chairs and lounges. You've tested the wind and sun and indicated on your plan where your windbreak should be and, if you are planning for shade, where your trellis, awning support, or shade trees will be. You've also marked off the areas you will use for flowers, potted shrubbery, or other greenery.

The next step is to decide what furniture you need and what style and kind is best for you. There's an endless variety nowadays, suited to every kind of outdoor-living need, and to individual tastes and pocketbooks. Available models range from elegant wrought- or cast-iron or aluminum garden furniture to inexpensive metal and wood pieces or folding deck and beach equipment.

If you are furnishing a porch off the living room and are working on a limited budget, consider at least one piece of furniture on which you can lie down. It might be one of those heavenly, comfortable, double chaise longues on wheels, or it might be a pair of simple couches with wooden frames, webbing, and foam-rubber mattresses. Wedge pillows at one end of an ordinary couch makes it ideal for lounging and reading. If the couches are placed longways against the wall or porch railing, a row of wedge pillows for back rests will convert them into sofas for seating several people. You will need at least two end tables to hold ashtrays, beverage glasses, magazines, and so on. Sometimes a large coffee table between the two chaises will serve this function. Reading lamps should be adjustable to various

168

▲

Terrace at back of house is ideal for outdoor dining. Paving and wall of brick; planting in shades of pink; weather-wise furniture.

▼

An outdoor living room paved in brick is terraced for sun and shade. The warm rhythm of brick repeats itself throughout this inviting spot.

▲ *A handsome and practical outdoor living room affords all the facilities for cooking, eating, and just relaxing. The dining and cooking unit is completely built-in—the table, stools, and cooking grills on brick base which is wired for electricity. An ingenious fence is composed of two rows of vertical boards placed to ensure good ventilation plus privacy. Lighting is concealed in shrubbery.*

170

heights so they may be used for reading lying down or sitting, for cards, or for general illumination. In some cases one of the new lighting "poles" with three or four fixtures attached will solve your lighting problems. On these poles, each lighting unit may be moved up and down and trained in the direction in which light is needed, or upward for general illumination.

If you must furnish your outdoor-living area on a limited budget, one of the best economies is to consider using standard captain's chairs (or director's chairs as they are sometimes called). These folding chairs come in painted or natural finishes with canvas seats and backs of various colors. They may be used indoors or outdoors, and you'll often find them in strictly nonbudget décor. Another good-looking budget idea is to make your own end tables, coffee table, and game or buffet table. This can be accomplished easily with metal legs, available in hardware stores today, that may be attached to various kinds of table tops or frameworks.

Another budget trick for an undercover porch is to refinish old discarded indoor pieces of furniture you may have, such as an old oak refectory table. Such a piece will look entirely different when it is painted white or bleached to a driftwood finish.

While most furniture that is suitable for an uncovered terrace can be used on an enclosed porch, the reverse is not necessarily true. For instance, elaborately cushioned rattan pieces should be used in protected areas and are ideal for a covered porch. The rattan frames of this furniture have usually been lacquered to resist moisture, and the fabrics used on the cushions should be water-repellent, unless your porch is completely glass-enclosed.

Wooden furniture can have an indoor-outdoor life, and pieces made of redwood or cypress can safely be left out in all weathers; but cushions, no matter how water-repellent the covering is, will fare better if they are brought in when it rains. You may also like some of the new furniture that combines wood or woven reed with wrought-iron supports. These pieces are easy to move around, have a light refinement of line that suits small space, and come in many soft colors.

There's also tubular metal furniture—both folding and nonfolding chairs and tables—combined with wood, woven reed or rattan, and with various fabrics. The tubular metal supports may now be had in metallic colors if you like, as well as brushed brass and the standard chrome.

Indoors or out, one of the most handsome styles of patio furniture is the wrought- or cast-iron variety. Most of this furniture is actually made of aluminum nowadays, which gives it far greater lightness and mobility. You will find it in elaborate traditional styles and in streamlined and restrained modern design; it may be had in white or a wide range of colors, including Antique-Florentine green.

Whatever kind of furniture you decide on, there are one or two things to remember. Most important, choose pieces that are easy to move around, particularly chaises and chairs. You'll want to be able to follow the sun or shade, without breaking your back pushing the furniture around. For this reason, chaises with back wheels are good, and light lounge chairs that are easy to get a grip on. A dining table with wheels at one end may also be convenient. And you will find a roll-about barbecue and bar cart a great joy. Or if you have a built-in barbecue, be sure to have a wheeled cart for serving, bringing supplies from the kitchen, and collecting dirty dishes.

Look for pieces of furniture that can do double duty: for instance, a dining table that can be used for games and small pull-up tables that can also be used for stools. If you intend to do a good deal of entertaining on your terrace, it is well to have a few comfortable folding chairs that can be stored in a tool house or a closet and brought out when needed. Plastic-covered cushions that can be piled up and used as hassocks or laid out flat to make a comfortable pad for sun bathing are another convenience.

How to Plan Your Colors

While we usually associate outdoor living with gay and cheerful colors, one of the first things to remember is that the outdoors itself is full of brilliant shades which will act as a foil for any colors you add. Therefore it is best to keep your own color scheme simple. One or two bright accent colors are usually more effective than a riot of primary shades.

In an open patio or terrace the colors you choose may depend a good deal on the style and general feeling of your house. If it is rustic and informal, with natural wood siding or fieldstone masonry, and your outdoor-living area is in keeping, you'll probably have chosen some simple metal or wood furniture suited to bright, clear colors. They may be primary shades of red, yellow, or blue, or clear, strong shades of burnt-orange, yellow-green, or gold.

If your house is more formal, with traditional lines or with brick masonry (plain or painted white) the colors you choose will be more subtle and sophisticated. One of the clear, strong pastels such as

▲ *A house built on a hill features a family room that's a deck with a breathtaking view. Riding high, deck's railings are open and angled the better to see. Furniture is simple, easily moved, and arranged in groups for reading or talking, eating, card-playing, and hobnobbing with treetops,*

173

cerulean-blue, geranium-pink, lettuce-green, or lemon-yellow, might be chosen for your seat pads and cushions or for an awning lining.

If you are decorating a covered porch that opens off your living or dining room, your color scheme should harmonize with the indoor room. You might want to use a lighter shade of one of the colors in the living room: for instance, if the room has a green rug, you might do the porch in a pale celadon-green. Or if there is quite a bit of blue, brown, or red in the living room, you might tie in the outdoor living area with the respective lighter shade—pale blue, beige, or pale coral-pink.

Sometimes the most effective treatment for such an area is to use a lot of white for floor, walls and furniture, with only small accents of color. Painting the ceiling a contrasting color is often dramatic, and minimizes the glare of brilliant sunlight. Cool colors are best for this: cerulean-blue, turquoise, soft medium green, and even battleship-gray or gunmetal. (These last two shades, however, do need to be offset by strong accents on the furniture and cushions, such as red or geranium-pink, sunflower-yellow or burnt-orange.)

In some cases the color you want can be brought to your outdoor living area best by the use of an awning or canvas tarpaulin that rolls down over a wooden or metal frame. Awning canvas comes in exciting colors these days, and can be installed on push-button-operated frameworks. Such a canopy can be as colorful as you want (or as conservative) and may provide the covered protection you need for an otherwise open terrace or patio. Canvas, lashed to a wood or metal frame with cord threaded through metal eyelets, may be used for a windbreak. In this way it can bring a spot of bright color into your patio.

A garden or beach umbrella is another means of bringing color into your patio. One of the large table umbrellas that tips with the sun is both a great comfort and a decorative asset in the average patio or garden. It can be lined with a contrasting color or a wonderfully gay floral print. Smaller adjustable umbrellas to screw on the back of your lounge chair or the chaise can be gay color additions too.

Upholstery and Fabrics for Outdoor Living

As the demand for outdoor living equipment has grown, the chemical and textile industries have worked hand in hand to produce moisture-repellent fabrics that are able to withstand long hours of strong sunlight. Most fabrics recommended for outdoor living have these qualities in varying degree. But remember, "water-repellent" does not mean "waterproof"; and even a plastic-coated fabric that is completely waterproof in itself, when used to cover chair cushions, will usually allow water to leak in at the seams if the cushions are left out in a driving rain. And even the best "sunfast" fabrics don't stand up forever in the strongest sunlight, though some of the new synthetic fabrics, even in light shades, are remarkably color fast.

There are many quick-drying fabrics of plastic-treated canvas or sailcloth which can be left out in all weathers without too much damage. Woven-nylon and woven-Saran webbing are also used for quick-drying seating. But generally speaking, your furniture (especially the cushions) will last longer if it can be kept under cover during stormy weather. If there's no covered place to put it, you'll do well to provide a plastic or rubber waterproof tarpaulin for all the furniture, or at least for the seat cushions.

For the most part the best upholstery material for seat pads and toss cushions is foam rubber. But many of the more luxurious types of furniture, such as rattan or wrought-iron lounge chairs and sofas, require cushions with innerspring construction or other materials that need moisture protection.

When you are choosing a fabric to cover a large area—such as a windbreak, an awning, or a shade—you usually have to make your selection from a small sample, so it is important to visualize how a broad expanse of the material will look. You want to be sure it doesn't clash with the colors around it. Cool colors—blue or green, green-and-white stripe, or a cool version of a "warm" color, such as citron-yellow lined with white—often work out best.

▼ *Terrace off living room, visible through window wall, provides space to sunbask, eat, and entertain in sunlit seclusion. Ingenious fence preserves ventilation.*

▼ *A secluded patio, girded by house and wall and shaded by a tree and overhead trellis, makes a pleasant spot to relax and entertain. Plants and decorative map add a personal touch.*

It's also well to remember when choosing a fabric that you may grow tired of a bold, splashy, too-insistent design. Generally speaking, if you want pattern on your terrace, a two-toned stripe, a plaid, or an evenly spaced geometric design will wear better psychologically than an overscale, overbright tropical pattern. On the other hand, a well-chosen floral or other patterned fabric may be just the touch needed to give sparkle to a covered porch or lanai adjoining a subdued living or dining room.

Lighting for Outdoor Living

A covered, screened, or glassed-in porch is lighted at night in very much the same way as an indoor room—with some general illumination, and special lighting where it is needed. Earlier in this chapter we mentioned a lighting "pole" as one of the ideal ways to get both general and local illumination. If you have an old-fashioned porch with a glary, depressing light in the middle of the ceiling, you can use a reflector under the bulb to cast the light upward to the ceiling for an indirect lighting effect, or make the fixture the outlet for a modern hanging lamp installed over a table. Modern ceiling lamps can be raised and lowered on a pulley, and some models move about the room on a track so they may be used in various places.

If your porch has old-fashioned wall brackets, you can cover these homely items with reflectors that throw the light back into the wall and give a diffused general lighting effect. If you use the porch for reading or cards, you'll want good concentrated light beside your chair, sofa, and card table. Portable lamps of adjustable heights can be adapted to either use and moved around as needed.

Even on a covered porch it is well to use plug-ins and wire cords designed for outdoor use, but in an open patio it is, of course, essential. For general illumination, you can have a light attached to the wall of your house or to a tree, or a special pole for such garden illumination. There are also low mushroom-shaped fixtures that can be staked into the ground wherever you want them to light a flight of steps, a flower bed, or a decorative pool. Special spotlights train light on the areas you will be using most, such as the barbecue counter; and of course the usual reading lamps (with outdoor cords) will provide illumination for you if you read outdoors in the evening. It's also possible while you have the electrician on the job to have him install wiring on the patio to accommodate a speaker from your hi-fi, and an outlet for plugging in the TV set. Don't forget that one of the prettiest kinds of outdoor illumination is old-fashioned candlelight. You can get all sorts of candle holders with hurricane shades for your dining table, or on iron standards to stick into the ground where you need them.

▲ *Dining room at rear of house can open wide onto porch-patio overlooking harbor to make one breezy recreation room. Glass jalousies make it snug in cold weather without blocking view. Furniture is light, modern.*

▶

Graceful wrought-iron furniture, rugged enough to stay outdoors and versatile enough to be used indoors, enlivens this tree-shaded terrace. The low, curved stone structure gives it a sense of privacy and provides extra seating space, shielded by trees, shrubbery, and plants.

Outdoor family terrace with a well-defined dining area, a place for cards or informal bar, done with light wrought-iron furniture, adds up to the biggest, least expensive, and happiest room of the house.

This paved terrace is defined by wooden benches. Planter boxes made of brick hold shrubs and flowering trees, adding pattern. The terrace, when viewed from inside this small modern house, further extends the apparent size of the living room.

Accessories, or the Little Things That Count

Often the small things set the personality or mood of your outdoor-living area. Perhaps it's a grouping of potted plants in interesting earthenware pots, or arranged in several plant holders. Or your plants may be combined with a lead garden figure, or with a bit of terra cotta or an old wooden sculpture. Or you may have a little fountain, or a birdbath against one wall. In an enclosed porch, bird cages hung at the four corners of the room proclaim the fact that you are a family of bird lovers. A ship's figurehead, a carved eagle, or a lavabo filled with flowers are other possible expressions of your personal tastes.

Outdoor ashtrays should be large, deep, and partly covered over so the wind will not blow the ashes away. Some people use containers of sand for burying all cigarette butts.

Dining-out accessories are as varied as you could wish. There are cotton, linen, and plastic cloths in all colors, place mats in straw, plastic, cotton, or heavy linen, and an endless assortment of colorful earthenware, plastic, or wooden dishes. Chafing dishes, food heaters, beverage glasses of all sorts are yours to choose from. And if you entertain at buffet suppers, be sure to have a supply of individual trays, so people can serve themselves easily. While you can use your regular table silver outdoors, it is better to have a set of stainless steel for such meals.

178

▲ *A rich red and white* toile de jouy *pattern, used against serene pale blue walls, carries out the French-provincial theme in this charming bedroom. The writing shelf and storage unit arrangement is an interesting modern note in an otherwise provincial décor.*

9 Bedrooms

Your plans for decorating a bedroom will depend, first and foremost, on whose room you are working on. If it's your own, the job is one thing; if it's for your teenage daughter or young son, the baby, grandma, or an overnight guest, it may be any of several other things.

The next consideration is: "What, besides sleeping, dressing, and undressing, will it be used for?" A bedroom may be used for study, play, reading, writing, sewing, work on a hobby. If it is used for relaxation, TV, or listening to records, it may double as an additional sitting room. Any or all of these possibilities will influence your planning and govern your choice and arrangement of furniture.

Of course, a bedroom is primarily a place for sleep, and the first requirements are comfort, quiet, and the possibility of shutting out light. But this is not all; in even the most streamlined room, storage for clothes, facilities for grooming, and enough space to move around in are fundamental. If you've a larger room you can add such other furnishings as a desk, comfortable chairs or a chaise longue, a sewing corner, bookshelves, TV, radio, extra reading lamps, and a breakfast or tea table. But in a room of average size or smaller, use fewer and more thoughtfully chosen pieces of furniture to avoid crowding and clutter. If closet space is inadequate, consider sacrificing some of your floor space to install a storage wall or built-in closets.

For furniture arrangement, begin by drawing a floor plan as you would with any other room. Place the beds first, if possible so that they do not face the windows. If you can't put the beds together, try arranging them at right angles against the walls at a corner of the room. Then indicate your storage pieces, drawn to scale on graph paper, and add extra pieces where you need them if you have enough space.

Meanwhile you will have been thinking about the style and mood you wish to create, whether traditional or modern, elegant or casual, frilly or tailored. Unless you are a bride starting from scratch, you will undoubtedly already have some pieces of furniture which must be incorporated into the plan.

Bedding Comes First

Never scrimp on your mattresses and box springs. Be sure they are right for each member of the family—that they are firm enough to hold the body without sagging and give uniform, buoyant support at every point. Some people prefer an innerspring mattress; others like one of foam rubber. People who like or need an extra firm mattress may want one of horsehair. Only you can decide which is most comfortable for you. When shopping for bedding, put your shyness aside and lie on the sample in the store to try it out. If possible, take other members of the family along to do the same thing.

Good pillows—whether of down, feathers, or foam rubber—and light, warm blankets are worth every penny you spend on them. If you must budget carefully, the place to economize is on the headboard or the bedstead. You can have your box springs mounted on legs or on a metal frame on wheels to which a headboard may be attached later.

Storage Comes Next

The average house is woefully lacking in adequate closet and storage space. This is especially true of the average master bedroom, where there is often one closet for both husband and wife. Even if there are two or more closets they may be badly planned with some space wasted and what space there is inappropriate for what you want to store (see chapter on closets and storage).

Inadequate closet room makes it all the more important for you to choose furniture for your bedroom which will give you the storage space you need. Almost every furniture manufacturer nowadays makes an assortment of flexible chest-of-drawer and storage units which can be arranged side by side or stacked one on top of the other. These come in many finishes, woods, and styles, and if your wall space is limited, you can get a maximum of storage space in a small area with a group of these units. If you already have a traditional dresser or chest that you will continue to use, a pair of small modular units may be used on either side of the bed as bedside tables to give you extra drawer space. Or a row of modular pieces may be placed under windows where traditional storage units would never fit.

182

▶ *A handsome ornate brass headboard is silhouetted against a white wall. The gold color is repeated in draperies, dust ruffle, and lamp shade. The colorful old-fashioned quilt together with simple furniture and antique accessories give this bedroom a charming countrified air.*

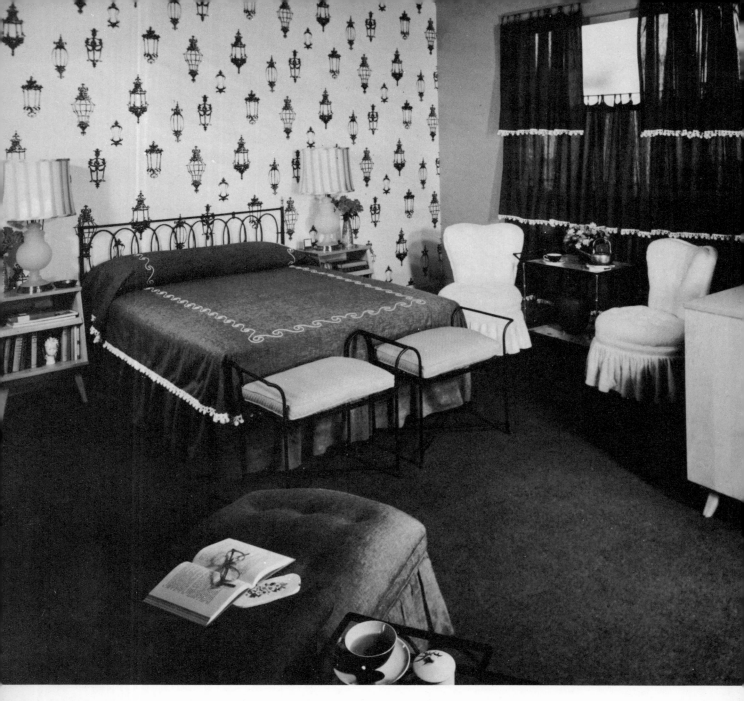

▲ *An intriguing wallpaper pattern of antique lanterns*
on one wall lends an air of gaiety to charcoal and
pink color scheme in this modern bedroom.

These modular units may be added to as your need for space increases, and they may be rearranged in different groupings as space in the room suggests. Some units are designed with drawers fitted to hold men's shirts and accessories, while others are styled for women's clothing. Many of them have space for hanging blouses or jackets and bins for hats, bags, shoes, and the like. One unit, which can be used as a dressing table, has a lift-up center section that contains a mirror and compartments for make-up and other grooming materials. Another conceals a small writing desk.

Other Furniture

One of the minor comforts of life in your bedroom is a bedside table of adequate size. This is especially important where there is to be a single table between twin beds. Ideally, it should be more than large enough to hold the lamp, telephone, ashtrays, vacuum container for water, books and magazines, and radio. Several drawers are a blessing too, for a box of tissues, the telephone book, and a heating pad. Most so-called bedside tables are too small for all this, so you will usually do better to look for what you want among occasional tables designed for living rooms.

Lounge chairs for the bedroom should be as well-constructed and comfortable as those in the living room. Usually, however, you will

▼ *An interesting arrangement of books, paintings, and decorative objects and handsome bedspread, embroidered in a bold design of leaves, lend pattern and color to this simple modern bedroom.*

want them to be lighter and smaller in scale. The so-called boudoir furniture you see in the stores is pretty and sized to fit the average bedroom space, but much of it is flimsy and will not wear well under hard usage. So be careful to look for quality here, especially if you expect to use your bedroom as a second sitting room.

If you have room for a small table for breakfast or to use for sewing and laying out work projects, it's a nice thing to have, but if space is insufficient, a sturdy folding table may be substituted. Such a table can be kept behind the drapery or in a closet when not in use. A hassock or bench at the foot of the beds if the room is large enough is a great convenience (and keeps you from sitting on the bed, too).

Mirrors are an important part of the furnishings of every bedroom, and many rooms are completely inadequate in this respect. At least two mirrors—a large one over the dresser and one of full length set in a doorframe—are absolutely necessary. If you can, have two full length mirrors arranged so you can see your reflection from all sides.

The Master Bedroom—Color and Background

The character of the furnishings and the color scheme you choose for your master bedroom are important factors in achieving the atmosphere you want.

If you want to create an atmosphere of quiet elegance, you'll look to the more formal traditional styles of eighteenth- and nineteenth-century England and France. Or some of the more stylized modern adaptations will appeal to you, with such accents as a modern brass headboard or marble-topped brass bedside tables.

This feeling of elegance will be enhanced by the choice of soft wall-to-wall carpet and fabrics with a refinement of surface texture, such as taffetas, satins, polished cottons, velvets, and velveteens. Restrained damasks, narrow stripes, graceful florals, and delicate tracery designs are good patterns for a formal bedroom. Walls can be either painted or papered with one of the more elegant wallpaper designs— a paper with a silklike weave, a rich flock paper, a damask pattern, a satiny tone-on-tone stripe, or perhaps one of the fantasy-type mural papers.

▶

A rich red wallpaper sets off dark mahogany furniture and gives a colonial bedroom an air of elegance. Red notes are repeated in trimming on swag valance, in dust ruffles, and in pillows.

186

A quaint allover wallpaper pattern helps disguise the many architectural breaks in this early-American bedroom. Canopied tester bed and double dresser fit compactly into a recess.

In such a room you will think first of soft, muted colors and pastels, for these are the colors we usually consider elegant in feeling. But don't assume that richer shades cannot produce an elegant room; if used properly, they can be just as effective in the traditional periods as are muted colors or pastels.

If you prefer an informal bedroom, you'll probably choose one of the provincial styles of furniture—early American, simple American eighteenth-century, French provincial—or some of the simpler modern designs.

With these, the colors you choose will be brighter and clearer than in a formal room. You can use almost any combination of colors: select one as your dominant color and one or two others as accents. Or, a very smart effect can be gained with a scheme worked out in varying shades of a single color. And a predominantly white scheme highlighted with black and bright accent colors can be very dramatic. For a casual country look gay colors and nubby tweedlike textures, patterns that are bright and informal—plaids, stripes, and small calico prints—are best. Your floor coverings should carry out the casual

▼ *Graceful white iron furniture and neatly spaced red and white wallpaper, underlined with soft blue carpet, give fresh appeal to countrified bedroom.*

188

▲   *In an age of tensions, this countrified bedroom has an atmosphere of luxury and repose. The sunny yellow in brick wallpaper, bedspreads, painted furniture, and sheer curtains makes it light and cheerful. Table-and-bench grouping in window suggests the luxury of breakfast and tea.*

▶ *Oriental mood is created in this feminine bed-room by Japanese-inspired hanging lamps, print over bed, and gold-printed draperies.*

▶ *The suave elegance of this bedroom is drama-tized by an unusual color scheme of crimson and gold in wallpaper and fabrics. Directoire furniture is mixture of black and fruitwood.*

► *The color scheme in this smartly tailored bedroom, taken from the striped fabric, repeats the beige in furniture and walls and orange tones in chairs and carpet.*

An unusual white four-poster bed is the focal point in this lovely traditional bedroom. The delicate blue and white striped paper makes a charming background for higher keyed blues.

feeling. You can choose a rug with a pepper-and-salt tweed effect, one with random stripes, a hooked design, or a braided effect. Or you can cover the floor with a room-size rug in a tweedy texture. Spatter floors are appropriate in this type of room; you can either spatter a painted floor with flecks of bright color or use one of the new spatter-dash smooth-surface floorings, such as vinyl or asphalt tile. Scatter or area rugs are also effective in this style of room, especially if it has a handsome wood or smooth-surface flooring. But don't forget room-size rugs and carpeting are among the best sound-deadening agents there are—an important factor in a bedroom, where quiet is essential for maximum comfort.

Whatever style of room you have, you'll want to keep it clear of all clutter except legitimate kinds—those that have their place in a room that is after all your own personal domain. It may be that you prize pictures—portraits of your relatives and friends, snapshots of the children and grandchildren, your husband's college team picture, or your

favorite travel photos. Try, however, to make them a decorative asset instead of a liability. Family pictures can be grouped together in a panel or mounted on a felt background. Or you can use interesting old frames or simple ones exactly alike.

Don't be afraid to mix periods in decorating your bedroom. If you have an old piece of furniture that's something of an eyesore but too good to abandon, you may include it. Maybe it will respond to a paint job, or can be bleached; curlicues and fancy legs can be amputated; sometimes just lining the drawers or shelves with a pretty wallpaper will give it an entirely new effect.

New Light on Bedrooms

Lighting the bedroom has a few special problems. There should be a switch to control the major source of light at the entrance door and another by the bathroom door if there is an adjoining bath. One of the most important lighting problems in the room is providing adequate light for reading in bed. If table lamps are used on the night tables, they should be high enough to spread the light so it falls on the book, but not in the eyes of the reader. An extra pin-up lamp for reading may be attached to the headboard or to the wall, but perhaps the most satisfactory bedside lamp is the hanging type which may be

▼ *The stunning Wedgwoodlike design in quilted chintz bedspread, headboard, and recess in which the bed stands, definitely dominates the bedroom. The background is kept simple with sheer curtains at window.*

▲

Against lovely printed curtains, the handsome dressing table, with graceful wrought-iron base, is the focal point in the bed-sitting room.

raised or lowered on a pulley and which can be swung from side to side as needed. Any bedside reading lamp, however, should be supplemented by general illumination in the room to avoid eyestrain.

Another important lighting requirement in the bedroom is for special illumination around the make-up mirror in the grooming area. Small "vanity lamps" are decorative here, but for real business you will need a bright but diffused light coming from both sides. The most satisfactory make-up lights are usually fluorescent tubes countersunk behind panels of diffusing glass around the mirror.

The Bed–Sitting Room

It is a real pleasure, if you own a house, to be able to invite relatives and friends to visit you. Since it's not always possible to have a bedroom set aside just for guests, the most practical guest room arrangement is to turn one of your rooms into a bed–sitting room. It might even double as a family room, study, hobby room, or TV room.

In a room of this kind your first consideration will be a convertible bed. Simple daybeds on legs give an easy and relatively inexpensive solution. Two of them may be placed end to end on a long wall, or set at right angles in a corner. A low table may be placed in the

▶ *A day bed, set in an alcove and treated like a French provincial bed, has storage space above and closets on either side, ideal arrangement for the bed-sitting room.*

▲ *The engaging double-dressing-table arrangement is ideal for two sisters who share a bedroom. The shelf is built-in, between two chests.*

195

corner or between them. If your space is inadequate for such arrangements you can find a large selection of sofa beds, or even chairs that unfold to make a single bed.

Other furnishings must be planned carefully to meet the needs of the room's double life. Be sure there will be an ample-sized bedside table and a good reading lamp beside the bed when it is made up for your guests. And by all means provide a luggage rack or a low bench for opening suitcases. A good mirror and light for make-up is essential even if there is a bath adjoining the room, and it is thoughtful to provide a closet or cupboard with hangers or a rack where clothes may be hung up. Little things for your guest's comfort may be kept together in a drawer ready to put out—a clock, ashtray, water carafe, tissues, aspirin, writing materials, pen, pencils, stamps, scissors, a pincushion with pin and threaded needles, scotch tape, and paper clips. A small private radio or a small television set will also add to your visitor's enjoyment, as will current books and magazines. Be sure there's an extra blanket or quilt in a drawer or on a closet shelf that can be reached easily, and don't forget a wastebasket. Your visitor will bless you, too, for dark shades or blinds to keep out the light if he wants to sleep late.

A painted "spool" headboard and bright quilted bedspread, made from a tablecloth with a Persian-inspired design, give character to an otherwise plain small modern bedroom.

196

▲ *A charming day bed cover, with a quilted top and scalloped edge over a dust ruffle, gives distinction to this small sitting-bedroom. The walls and carpet are a muted turquoise. Crimson, turquoise, and white plaid is used on chair.*

If you are fortunate enough to have a real guest room, furnishings can be simple and need not be expensive, but a comfortable bed and the little things listed above are essential. Besides the items already mentioned, a guest room should have at least one comfortable chair—either an upholstered small lounge chair or a rocker—for relaxation. A gay wallpaper will give the room a furnished and inviting look even if furniture is kept to the bare essentials. Sometimes it is effective to put the wallpaper on the ceiling, paint the wall a plain color, and repeat the colors of the paper in the rug or the bedspreads. If you decide to paper the ceiling, be sure to use an allover pattern without a strong direction in the design.

A half-tester bed, set off with a draped canopy bordered with a quaint print, and a handsome crocheted bedspread with pleated dust ruffle of same print, is the focal point in traditional bedroom.

This built-in dressing table, fitted under a window, has compact make-up box set in between storage cupboards. Graceful moldings and curved valance carry out eighteenth-century French feeling.

Closets Are a Blessing

It would seem that when you build a house, it should be simple to plan enough closets. Whether this is or is not the case, most of us have to live in houses somebody else planned—usually a somebody who obviously had very few worldly goods and practically no wardrobe. If you have a closet that must be used by two people, you can sometimes increase the use you will get from this space by installing double-decker rods for such short garments as men's jackets and suits or blouses and skirts. Trousers and longer dresses will usually need a rod of the average height (about six feet). Special hardware is available for hanging garments on the closet door, and there are racks for shoes, ties, belts, and bags that help you to use every inch of space.

Even a large closet, however, if it is arranged with imagination, can give you more usable space than you may realize. A small chest set under the rod where short garments are hung will give you storage space for small articles such as sweaters, shoes, hats, bags, and the like.

If you are remodeling, you can often obtain a great increase in usable space both inside the closet and in the bedroom by removing the old swing-out doors and substituting sliding panels. If you have a few square feet of floor space you can spare on either side of the windows, you might consider installing some of the prefabricated closets that are on the market nowadays. These will give you extra hanging and shelf space at comparatively little expense.

▲ *A modern background, with one wall of grasscloth, makes a pleasing setting for simple maple furniture mixed with peasantlike painted pieces.*

◀

All the personal comforts for repose and enjoyment are expressed in this warm, friendly bedroom with a countrified air.

201

10 Bathrooms

Your bathroom can have as much personality and individuality as any other room in your home—an effect which can be achieved with a few changes at little cost. To be practical, it should be a workmanlike room, and everything in it should be within easy reach.

First, consider its needs. Probably the most neglected feature in any bathroom concerns storage space and a place to put small articles. The usual medicine chest hardly ever provides sufficient space for storing articles used in the bathroom. Built-in storage cabinets with counter tops to put things on are the best solution. Also, a make-up counter or a dressing shelf is practical if you haven't a dressing table in your bedroom. And, of course, it is important to have good lighting.

If you have to rely on one small bathroom, your first requirement is to make it seem larger. Painting the walls and ceiling a pretty, light color, or covering the walls with a light, airy patterned wallpaper, and perhaps installing a large mirror are a few simple tricks for creating an illusion of space. Your next consideration should be the storage problem. The built-in cabinets described above installed along one wall will hold such articles as towels, cleaning equipment, and possibly soiled clothing. Counter tops can be used like tables for small articles you want to keep on hand, and one section might be used as a make-up counter. On the other hand, if you haven't a long wall space for a row of storage cabinets, consider counter tops with storage space below built in on either side of the basin. You could add a cupboard with two doors to hide the pipes under the basin and provide space for storing cleaning equipment.

◀

Tiled partition, in bold plaid design, braided rug, eyelet embroided curtains, and quaint accessories give this distinctive bathroom an old-fashioned countrified feeling.

If you plan to remodel your bathroom, investigate the new compartmented bathroom fixtures. Some of these modern, compact units are prefabricated and come equipped with a sunken wash bowl, with counter tops on each side and a clothes hamper and storage space under the counter tops. If you have a traffic problem, consider installing two basins.

Color Schemes

A new color scheme or even a few new decorative touches can often do as much to give your bathroom a new look as more elaborate redecoration. There are many clever and inexpensive tricks for achieving a new atmosphere. For example, if the walls and floor in your bathroom are attractive and in good condition, you might cover the ceiling with a gay wallpaper, or hang a charming scenic paper that picks up the colors in the room on one wall. You could repeat the major color of the wallpaper in a bath rug or in the new, relatively inexpensive and thoroughly practical cotton carpeting now available, as well as in towels.

If you plan to use a completely new color scheme for your bathroom, start by choosing a single favorite color, and use the color wheel as a guide for the selection of other colors within one of the three color harmonies. If you find it difficult to choose a color scheme, study the illustrations in this book; you might find colors you like enough to adopt.

Aside from obvious considerations of color harmony, an important feature in today's bathroom is a theme or a mood to give it personality. You can choose any colors you like, as long as they are in keeping with the atmosphere. For example, if your bathroom has old-fashioned fixtures, such as a bathtub with claw and ball feet, it might suggest a Victorian theme. In accord with the Victorian feeling, you might use a quaint floral wallpaper design such as a bouquet of violets with green leaves on a white background. The floor could be covered in a green marbleized smooth-surface flooring, and white ruffled window curtains would be appropriate. To further carry out the Victorian mood, you could use violet towels hung on ornamental brass rings, and arrange a collection of old amethyst glass bottles and jars on a white hanging shelf. Small pots of African violets, placed in a row on the window sill, would add an unusual touch.

▶

Grained cypress planks, with brick painted white, are used here for new walls in bathroom just remodeled. Coordinated fabrics for towels, curtain, and shower curtain are patterned in "blossoms and bows."

If your bathroom opens into your bedroom you can establish a feeling of continuity between the two rooms by repeating the bedroom color scheme in the bathroom. For example, the bedroom might have light citron-yellow walls with turquoise accents in the floral draperies, small chair, and blankets. In the bathroom, you might reverse this scheme and use light turquoise as the dominant color (for wall, floor, and fixtures) and citron-yellow as the accent color (in towels, bath rug, and shower curtain).

On the other hand, you may want your bathroom to have a masculine look, with perhaps a dominant dark color and bright accents. For example, if riding is the favorite sport of your family, you could carry out this theme in your bathroom. You might hang old hunting prints on your walls, and use them as the basis for your color scheme. The walls could be painted a muted green or covered with a small geometric wallpaper in tones of green. The floor might be a dark green strié smooth-surface flooring. Red accents to add sparkle might be used in towels, bath rug, and shower curtains, as well as in the hunting prints.

Above all, avoid such old clichés as an insipid pastel color scheme, or motifs such as seashells, fish, and water lilies in either wallpaper or shower curtain. Try to give your bathroom an individual theme or mood. The inspiration might come from a wallpaper, a shower curtain, a towel design, or from a collection of old prints. Your bathroom may be oriental, or modern, or it may have a luxurious

▶

Two-toned blue ceramic tiles set in stripes give a fresh clean look to a bathroom that even children can't clutter up. Toilet, tub, and basin are compactly grouped.

206

eighteenth-century French feeling; choose any style that suits your fancy. Whatever you do, make this room as attractive and distinctive as any other in your home.

Floors

Since a hard-surface flooring is easier to clean and maintain than a wood floor, you might use vinyl or asphalt tile, rubber tile linoleum, or a ceramic tile. If you want to give your bathroom floor a luxurious feeling, you can use washable cotton or nylon carpeting. This can be cut in sections and taped together on the underside. The sections can be easily removed and put in the washing machine. When dried, the sections can be taped together as before.

To give a smooth-surface flooring more warmth and interest, consider using an attractive bath rug. It might be unusually handsome by virtue of its lovely color, or it might be a novelty shape that carries out a motif in your bathroom, such as a huge strawberry, a round clock, or a butterfly.

Fabrics

A shower curtain, of course, should be of washable and water-proof material, such as plastic or specially treated silk or cotton.

◄

A view of bathroom opposite, showing one wall devoted to laundry department, with washer-dryer and two pull-out hampers for soiled clothes. Counter above is handy for sorting.

*Cool blues and greens of fixtures and furnishings
lend enchantment to a bathroom that has practical
easy-care features. Scrubbable, wood-patterned canvas covers the walls, shower enclosure is lined with
plastic wall tile.*

▲ *A seafarer dreamed up this bathroom, complete
with ship's clock. Sleek and streamlined as a yacht,
it is also gay and warm with its wallpaper of colorful ensigns and its ocean-going lantern.*

209

The shower curtain and window curtains may be either of the same material or of different ones. For example, you might have a plastic shower curtain with a bold design, while the window curtains might be a washable cotton or a sheer synthetic material in a solid color. The dressing table stool pad might be covered in a bright accent color, but the cover should be removable and washable.

Lighting

The lighting in your bathroom should be both practical and attractive. Often a new look can be achieved in an old bathroom by simply replacing stereotyped lighting fixtures either with modern ones or with attractive, decorative fixtures. Two brackets, one on each side of a mirror, and a ceiling fixture will adequately light the average bathroom. The brackets might be fluorescent tubes, either shielded or unshielded, or they might be attractive old fixtures with incandescent bulbs. (Incandescent bulbs should always be shielded; for a bathroom, a translucent material is sufficient shielding.) One or more recessed lighting units make effective ceiling fixtures, but they are quite expensive unless the ceiling, as in many new houses, has been planned for recessed lighting. For a less expensive ceiling fixture, hang an incandescent bulb or a fluorescent tube shielded with an attractive translucent covering close to the ceiling, or use a decorative hanging fixture such as an old oil lamp or a hanging bubble light.

If your mirror extends over a wash basin and a dressing counter or shelf, it can be amply lighted either with a long, shielded fluorescent fixture attached to the ceiling, or with two rows of concealed fluorescent lighting. The lighting of the mirror will be more effective if the counter tops or basin below are a light color.

Accessories

In addition to the use of paint, wallpaper, flooring, fabrics, and appropriate colors, unusual and interesting accessories can be employed to make your decorating theme complete.

Even such common items as towels, bath mat, shower curtain, hamper, and wastebasket, if they are distinctive, will give your bathroom an unusual touch. You can add to these other accessories that will give an extra fillip to your bathroom. You might choose such objects as a grouping of pictures, a collection of apothecary jars, glass candy jars to hold soap, cotton pads, and lotions, or unusual soap dishes. Today you can find all kinds of unusual bathroom fixtures (including reproductions of the antique styles) such as brass

▲ *The long counter top with storage cabinets below provides ample space in this small bathroom for lavatory and dressing table. Mirrored wall above counter gives it a spacious feeling.*

▲ *A feminine bathroom done in shades of pink has two convenient features in completely separate toilet and big linen closet behind shuttered doors. Curtains are coordinated with wallpaper.*

▶

The bathroom is one place in which you can indulge your decorating whims. A gay mural over the tub picks up the rose and vivid blues of the décor, re-echoed in the Moorish-type tile wall with its shelf convenient for soap, bath oils.

dolphin faucets, old ceramic basins decorated with border designs or with allover motifs, and unusual fixtures for hanging towels.

You can find any kind of accessories you need to carry out the theme or mood in your bathroom. The search requires imagination and a little ingenuity, but it can be lots of fun.

The Powder Room

If there isn't space for two completely separate bathrooms in your home or if your budget is limited, you can divide a large hall closet and make a tiny powder room out of one half of it. It will be invaluable as an extra wash-up place for the children, or for your friends when they come to dinner.

A powder room may be as gay and whimsical as you like. Since such a room is usually tiny, the gayest and giddiest décor never becomes tiring. An important item here is a make-up shelf (even if it must be installed above a wash basin) or a small dressing table with a well-lighted mirror above it. You should provide powder and other cosmetics. A wash basin, of course, is a must for a powder room.

There are many new toilet and lavatory combinations available that are small in size and operate quietly. This is most important, especially if your powder room is close to the living room or dining room.

One relatively inexpensive way of decorating a powder room is to use a gay, whimsical wallpaper, and cover the floor with either a smooth-surface flooring or a cotton or nylon carpeting. For example, you might use a wallpaper design of amusing cartoon figures in black outline on a white ground. One bright color, such as azalea pink or a sharp green could be used for both ceiling and floor, and the hand towels could be black combined with the bright color of ceiling and floor.

If you can't have a completely separate powder room, an unused space such as a recessed end of the entrance hall might be converted into a powder nook. You might cover the walls of the area with a gay wallpaper and use a small dressing table with a mirror and a stool, or install a make-up shelf with a drawer below and a mirror above. The mirror can be lighted with either decorative brackets on each side or an attractive down light hung from the ceiling. A pair of folding doors, such as louvered doors, would provide privacy.

▶

The fresh look of shamrock-and-white shower curtains, and the spanking white lambrequin, green-edged, give smart distinction to a bathroom whose accessories reflect the taste and imagination of the owner.

▲ *Old-fashioned bathroom fixtures can assume an attractive, well-bred air with a warm color scheme and a choice of stylish accessories. Orange and soft-green towels accent brown of damask paper.*

sampler is an attractive addition to an early-
merican bathroom featuring a weathervane towel
ack, towels with crocheted bands and fringe. The
g is crocheted, too.

▲ Walls and basin counter of this bathroom are blue-
green tile. Sliding doors of translucent glass enclose
shower and tub. Every surface has easily wiped,
glazed finish.

11 Children's Rooms

Every child derives great satisfaction from having a room he can call his own.

It is never too early to begin to teach a child to appreciate and care for his possessions and to develop a sense of orderliness. Even if two children share the same room, you can make plans taking into consideration the activities of each child.

If your children are old enough to have ideas of their own, take them into your confidence and find out their likes and dislikes before you decorate their rooms. If you give a child an attractive room with colors and furnishings he can admire and love, it will help him to develop his tastes and to learn orderliness, for he will cherish his own possessions.

Remember that children are active and even the sturdiest room may be turned into a shambles, so keep it simple. It's best when you select furniture to plan for the future, because children soon outgrow the usual nursery furniture. The furniture should be lightweight, so that it can be moved around easily, but sturdy. Beds, of course, should be durable, and a good mattress should be a first consideration. Be sure to include storage space for clothes, toys, and the endless paraphernalia that children collect. Children also need a work-play-hobby table or a desk at a convenient height. Place the beds, chests, table, and other furniture to allow as much of the floor space as possible for a play area.

◄ *Yards of organdy, painted secondhand furniture,*
are inexpensive ingredients for this baby's bower.
Draped wicker bassinet is lined with quilting.

In order to avoid crowding and clutter, it's a good idea to make a drawing of a floor plan on graph paper as you would for any other room. Place the largest pieces first, such as the bed, storage pieces, and play table, and then add the smaller pieces.

Color Schemes

Since children love color and color is cheap, choose colors that are fresh and gay. Many people select color schemes (especially for younger children's rooms) composed of insipid pastels. Don't forget that most children like bright, crisp colors.

A good rule to follow is to keep your color scheme simple, using no more than perhaps three colors—one less intense color for the largest areas, and one or two bright accent colors in the smaller areas. And there is no necessity for making a girl's room delicate and fluffy; it can be as modern and compact as a boy's, but the colors used should be ones that appeal to a girl. Girls usually like light but clear colors, such as pink, blue, light blue-green, and yellow; while boys favor blue, red, and other masculine colors. For example, if your daughter's preference demands a yellow background, you could pep it up with a clear, cerulean-blue accent color or, if she prefers pink, with accents of bright rosy-red. Your son, on the other hand might like blue with dashes of bright red, or a neutral color, like beige, with bright accents of orange and citron-yellow. You'll find many ideas for color schemes in this chapter.

Furniture

For a younger child's room, you'll need a bed (most children's beds have rails to keep the child from falling out of bed), a chest to hold small articles of clothing, a storage place for toys and collections, a play table (or shelf), and small chairs. Since children like to make things, a fairly large, low table or a wide built-in shelf for this kind of work is almost a necessity. The chairs for the table or shelf should be a comfortable height and size for the child.

When you shop for furniture, look for pieces that can be used as the child grows older. The choice in juvenile "grow-up" furniture is rather limited, but there are good designs available in simple modern and provincial styles. Most children's furniture is sold in the infant's department in stores, but you can find pieces of small-size furniture, such as unit storage cabinets and low tables and chests suitable for a child's room in the regular furniture department. You may choose

▲ *A morning-glory print for café curtains, valances, and swag set the color scheme—soft pinks and blues—for this baby's room. The precious old-time cradle and rocker whisper of peaceful slumber. Perfect* poudreuse *for baby is the old-fashioned shaving-stand-and-mirror. Wardrobe has room for linen, small clothes, and row of baby's shoes.*

finished furniture or unpainted pieces that can be lacquered a bright color or left the natural color and waxed. Because there is a wider choice of colors, finishes, and designs in these adult pieces, you may find that they will give your child's room more individuality than would a matching set of juvenile furniture. Above all, don't be lured into buying badly designed, commonplace, small-size juvenile furniture decorated with coy bunnies, flowers, or circus figures. Your child will soon outgrow such furniture and grow tired of the decorations.

Be sure to plan for two beds, because one of the joys of childhood is spending the night with a friend. Daybeds or bunk-beds (the kind that can be separated to form two beds) are most practical. If the room is small, they can be treated as sofas and arranged along one wall with a table or low chest placed between them, or placed at right angles in one corner of the room. Also provide a study-hobby table, a desk, a chair or two, and plenty of shelves and storage space.

If you are planning a teen-ager's room, remember that teen-agers are very gregarious. They love to gather together to play their favorite records, or to pursue hobbies. Because they like to entertain friends in their own rooms, the most comfortable and practical arrangement is a sitting-bedroom with daybeds (or sofa beds) instead of conventional beds.

In a small bed–sitting room with two daybeds you will need space-saving furniture, such as built-in or flexible chests for storage, shelves for collections or records, and a compact study area. The study area might be a combination of storage units and desk. There should also be seating pieces of some kind. For study and work, a chair is best. However, teenagers love low stools or floor cushions when they are playing records or entertaining their friends.

Even with a limited budget you can make a child's or teenager's room attractive with a little ingenuity and imagination. You can buy well-designed unpainted furniture that can be painted to harmonize with the room or left natural and waxed. Or, if you have odds and ends of "white elephants," take off the ugly curlicues and paint the pieces all the same color—preferably a color that blends with the walls. If some member of your family is handy at making things, there is precut "do-it-yourself" furniture with simple instructions, and there are also patterns for making your own furniture.

▶

A little girl's room has an inexpensive chest and headboard painted blue, box spring and mattress for a bed. Glazed chintz curtains and a spread are vivid accents, green and turkey red.

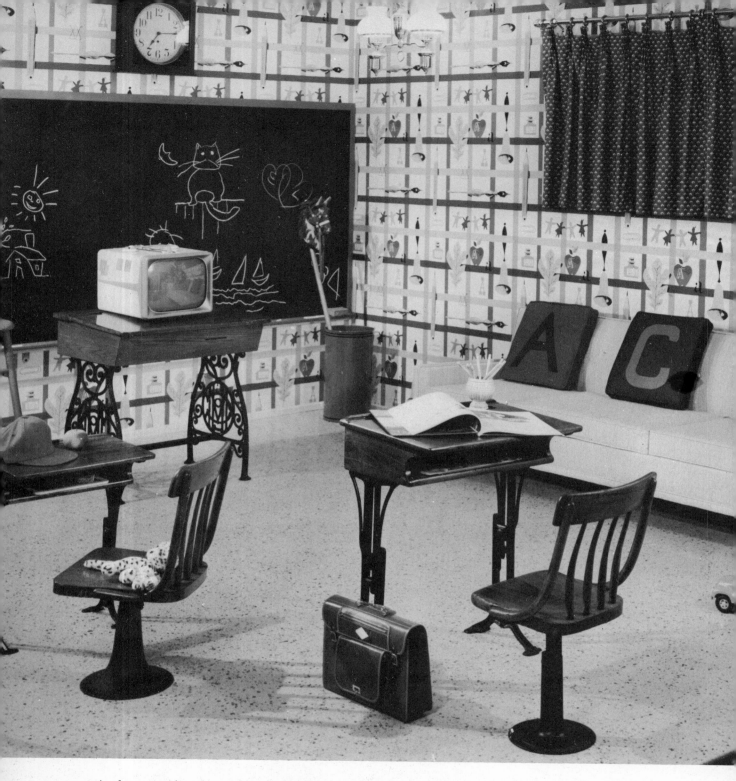

▲ *A playroom for three children demonstrates the wisdom of buying sturdy furniture, indestructible flooring, well-designed wallpaper. The schoolroom atmosphere of this room is softened by its lively walls and café curtains, toys and television set, world maps for window shades, its warm colors. Experimenting with blackboard fantasies develops taste and imagination.*

▶ *Another view of playroom shows toy bins for three. Old-fashioned school desks provide individual play areas. Glassed-in terrace adds its decorative charm.*

Walls

If you want solid-colored walls, be sure to use a good washable paint, or one of the scrubbable wallpapers that now come in beautiful solid colors.

To give an individual touch to a child's room, consider papering the ceiling in a small allover pattern like a sprinkling of stars, tiny polka dots, or a posy design. Or, you might cover the walls with a narrow calico stripe or small polka dots, and paint the ceiling; or cover one wall with a wallpaper showing a map of the world, musical notes, or forest animals.

Fabrics

Washable fabrics are best for children's rooms because children of all ages give their rooms hard wear. There is a wide selection of washable fabrics to choose from, including cottons, man-made fibers, blends of different kinds, and plastic fabrics. You can find almost any color, design, or texture that you want, so try to choose patterns that your child can grow up with, especially if you can't change

▼ *Twin wicker beds are for two little girls in room that converts easily to teenage tastes: peg-board for dolls, blue rose-print draperies, hanging lamp apiece.*

226

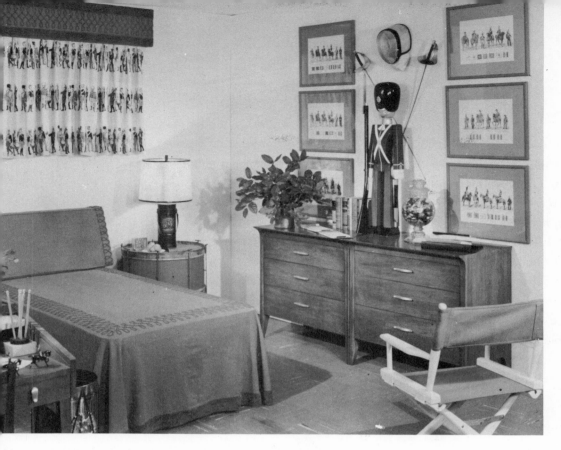

▲ *"Guardsman" is designed for a boy with a soldierly*
bent. Curtains are blue and red guardsman print.
Floor is blue, spread brilliant red.

the decoration in his room every year or so. Small checks or plaids, narrow stripes, polka dots, neat florals, evenly spaced geometric designs, or quaint toiles (provincial scenes in tints and shades of one color) are some of the patterns that stand the test of time in a growing child's room. Cute nursery rhymes and coy animal designs are all right when a child is very young, but he soon grows tired of cute designs.

Here are some ideas for a limited budget. Make your daughter's room pretty and feminine by using ordinary muslin sheets in a lovely color for a draped dressing table skirt, a bedspread or dust ruffles, and curtains for the window. Use a trimming of ruffles, ball fringe, or eyelet embroidery to add a decorative touch. Sheets require little sewing because of the wide expanse of seamless fabric, and they wear well through constant washing. For a boy's room, you'll find such colorful, washable fabrics as denims, corduroy, and cotton tweeds both effective and inexpensive. And try Venetian blinds or split wood blinds painted in stripes for a boy's room instead of curtains.

Floors

Floor coverings in children's rooms should be chosen carefully. Ideally the flooring should be durable and easy to clean; linoleum, vinyl, and asphalt tiles will withstand spilled liquids and rough usage. Children are active little people and their floors take a terrible beating not only from constant scuffing but also from such childhood games as running heavy toys-on-wheels back and forth across the floor or "building" with a hammer. (Most children use the floor for a work space and more often than not, the hammer connects with the floor rather than the nail.)

If you want rugs to add warmth and color to the flooring, choose washable cotton or nylon rugs. Small sizes, such as 3- by 5-foot rugs, can be laundered at home in a washing machine, and larger sizes can be commercially laundered.

Lighting

One of the most important considerations when you are planning a child's room is proper lighting. There should be good general illumination, with the switch within reach of the child, and specific lighting for certain areas. Portable table and floor lamps are less practical than built-in or hanging lamps, for they can be tipped over by a small child. Down lights, attached to either the wall or the ceiling, can serve as both general illumination and specific lighting. You might use pulley lamps, which can be raised and lowered, or immobile lamps, such as those made in clusters of three or four small hanging lights with shades. Not only are hanging lights safest and most practical when your child is small, they can continue to serve him as he grows up.

A low night light is desirable for a baby's room or for very young children; it is especially useful for late night trips. A pulley lamp is a practical, economical, and space-saving light for nighttime use. Since it plugs in like a portable lamp, it may be moved to any part of the room. Most pulley lamps have top and bottom diffusers to eliminate glare.

Remember that good lighting is most important for young eyes, so avoid a glaring ceiling fixture for general illumination and inadequate children's lamps that are designed for cuteness rather than for good lighting.

▲ *Installed between two prefabricated closets, a counter serves as a play area while the child is small, as a dressing table later. The louvers of the closet doors are repeated on shutters and chests. The wallpaper, used sparingly throughout the room, has well-designed Mother Goose motifs.*

229

◄

Young baseball fan's room with secondhand gym lockers and bench in blue of "hobby" wallpaper (not shown); other walls of wood-patterned paper. Formica-topped shelves, one supported by chests, act as counter and shelf. Wall brackets are bat racks; café curtains are made out of bath towels. Trundle bed rolls out and up for sleeping.

231

Accessories

When the color scheme, basic furnishings, and lighting are worked out, it is time to decide on accessories; try to choose things that children like to have around them.

Most children are collectors at heart; at all ages they like to display their collections, toys, and souvenirs on open shelves. You can use built-in shelves, or shelves attached to a wall or chest. If the shelves are attached to a wall, they should be within the child's reach.

Children's collections may start with a strange assortment of such objects as birds' eggs, birds' nests, bits of drift wood, stones, shells, odd bits of colored glass, miniature dolls, and small stuffed or earthenware animal figures. Until your child reaches an age of reason, his collections may be a disorderly array indeed; but if you show an interest in his collections and guide him as he grows, he may eventually acquire a very tasteful and interesting collection, such as one of rare shells, interesting drift-wood shapes, or beautiful butterflies.

Your child will enjoy a large bulletin board or a pegboard where he can hang trophies, snapshots, cutouts, and mementos of all kinds, and it is good for a child to have his treasures tacked to a board rather than lying around helter-skelter or dumped in drawers. Another constructive idea, even at nursery stage, is to expose your child to good art; children are best able to respond to art if they have it around them when they are young. You might begin with subjects in old nursery rhymes, or any childlike theme that has good drawing and color. Or, you can get good reproductions of paintings by well-known artists showing children or a mother and child. Later on, you could change to more sophisticated subjects; many children like modern art, so don't discount good modern painting and drawings.

Then, of course, since a child likes to display paintings and sketches that he has done himself, help him plan a space where he can exhibit his creations. You may find that you have a budding artist in your family.

The striking wall hanging suspended from the molding is a beach towel, and striped towels with brass clips serve as curtains. The bright red bedspread carries out the gaiety of the color scheme, and the college furniture is augmented by a comfortable folding deck chair and two tables which double as stools.

▲ *Here's a delightful room for a teenage girl. The couch converts into a double bed for slumber parties, the closets are prefabricated but look built-in. The curtains and bedspread, in an old-fashioned print, were ready-made; extra one makes the canopy. A coordinated fabric was used to cover the walls. The four-poster, early-American chest, and chairs fit serenely into modern setting.*

234

▲ *Airy café curtains hung in tiers on big brass rods keynote this child's room. Canopies and bedspreads, wallpaper, and even the pattern traced on little chest are coordinated, in red with white.*

▶

Crisp glazed-chintz curtains with deep ruffles are used in this child's room. The fresh flower pattern is repeated in a matching wallpaper used beneath dado and to frame window and door.

Naturally, toys and assorted treasures will be decorative accessories enough; but—on the practical side—it's a good idea to have at least one commodious wastebasket, which will help your child to be neat. Also, it is almost essential to have a small radio or television set in your child's room if you want to preserve your sanity, because most children turn on the radio and TV at full blast.

You will find many helpful ideas for children's rooms in the illustrations. And remember that it's good common sense to make your children's rooms attractive and comfortable so that they won't want to overrun the rest of the house or be constantly visiting their friends' homes. Also, it gives a child a feeling of security to have a room he can enjoy and respect.

◀

The sons of this household share room that provides space for two sets of treasures. Storage wall has two chests with plank stretched across for play space—all painted green of chair and peg-board. Green blankets on double-decker bunk act as spreads.

Boy's room, called "Safari," appears to have a built-in storage wall. These are in fact stacked units—chests, shelves, cupboards. Ocelot-stenciled bedspreads are washable, fur-like, sold over dress-goods counters. Curtains are of sailcloth.

239

▲ This sturdy and attractive bedroom, shared by two boys, provides ample space for treasures and books. The two four-drawer storage chests have a long plank stretched between for play and work. Chest assembly, chair, and pegboard are painted green; chintz curtains are red.

◀

Sports equipment and souvenirs, attached to a pegboard hung from molding by belts, set the mood of a bedroom of a travel-minded girl. Color scheme of tints and shades of coral, accented with blue, provides a pretty contrast. Under glass-topped desk are other personal mementos.

241

12 Storage and Closets

At the top of every list of complaints about today's houses and apartments is the lack of adequate storage and closet space. On the surface this complaint appears to be an odd one. Modern clothes— both men's and women's—require only a fraction of the closet space the wardrobes of thirty or forty years ago demanded, and elaborate tea and coffee services, numerous sets of dishes, and large supplies of table and bed linens are no longer used. Why then this persistent demand for storage space?

The problem is that family activities have broadened and possessions of all descriptions have multiplied. For example, former luxury items have become common household articles in almost every home; thus, there is a need for new kinds of storage space other than closets. While it is true that a broom and a mop can be put in a small closet for cleaning materials, a vacuum cleaner with all its attachments requires a different kind of storage space; a similar need is created by all the new types of electrical gadgets used in the kitchen. Hobbies,

Feminine, elegant, a louvered storage wall includes closets for hanging, shelves for shoes, and tier of storage units at ceiling level. A wide dressing-table counter spreads across three sections of drawer space.

games, and outdoor activities have been adopted by millions of people, and all of the articles needed for these pastimes must be stored someplace. But where to keep them? Where are we to store the barbecue sets, tricycles, skis, golf clubs, and tennis rackets, or the record albums, record players, and the enormous number of books that people are buying? The list is endless and it keeps growing.

The solution is storage space for particular articles. There are two kinds of storage units: those that are custom-designed and built-in to suit the requirements of the individual, and ready-made storage units that may be purchased in stores.

Most manufactured storage pieces for the home are designed to have a built-in look and there is, fortunately, a wide variety of sizes and of materials, finishes, and combinations to choose from. For example, if, in a small living room, you need storage space for games, magazines, card tables with folding chairs, and so on, as well as a place to put a television set, a record player, and books, you can find attractive unit storage pieces that will meet these requirements.

Eyelet embroidery edges shelves of closet below. Arrangement of shelves permits the storing of most-used pieces at easy levels, extra blankets above. Cupboard holds bathroom supplies.

▶

Well-organized linen closet has compartments sized to hold folded sheets, pillow cases, towels. Section at top is for bath cosmetics, at bottom for quilts, blankets, pillows, bedspreads.

◀

Three-closet arrangement in bedroom gives doors double duty: Far left, the wife's closet has a hinged section for shoes; the middle door holds husband's ties, shoes; the third has long mirror.

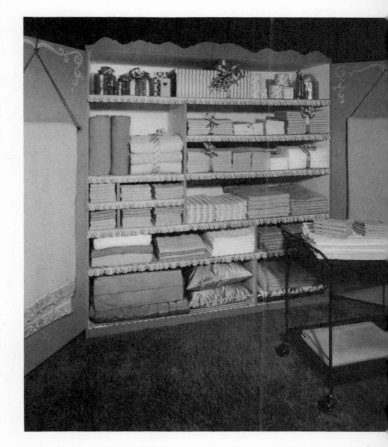

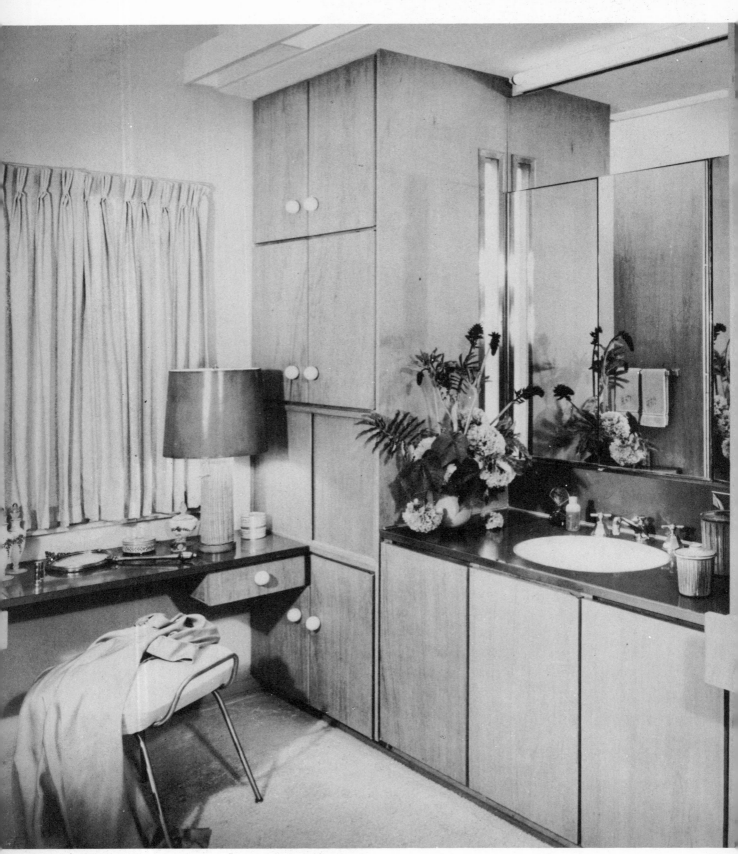

Modern dressing room—bath is equipped with handsome drawers and cupboards arranged around the basin counter to make a decorative wall pattern, contribute a wealth of storage space. Adjoining bedroom shares décor of pale wood paneling.

A corner built-in for storage takes into consideration a woman's wardrobe and accessories. Smooth sliding doors conceal hat boxes above, hanging space below, chest, and shoe-pockets.

Most storage furniture is contemporary in design, but many pieces have such an elegant, refined look (by virtue of fine wood, often combined with such materials as brass or leather and with delicate hardware) that they may be combined with fine traditional furniture as well as with modern styles.

Storage Furniture and Shelving

Basically, any storage unit is a rectangular box. Individual variations include the cabinet type, with compartment trays and shelves enclosed by doors; units with a series of drawers; styles having a drop front with inner compartments to form a desk, or the bookcase-type unit of open shelves for storing books, magazines, and decorative objects.

Wall Storage

Since many rooms lack floor space for free-standing storage cases, cabinets and shelves have been designed for wall mounting. The simplest and least expensive method for hanging shelves is to attach adjustable slotted metal strips and brackets to the walls to support the shelving or small cabinets. Most stores now carry these metal strips, brackets, and shelving.

Room Dividers

Because of the lack of wall space in so many contemporary houses, where rooms that in traditional architecture would have been separated by walls now often open into each other, a totally new piece of furniture has been developed. It is called a *room divider*. As a piece of furniture, a room divider is hard to describe in traditional terms. It is free standing and compartmented on both sides. Although a room divider often provides both cabinet and shelf space, it could hardly be

Individually engineered by a woman: Closet spaced for shoes and handbags, blouses, dresses. Doors are louvered for ventilation, swing to clear thick carpet for dust-proof closing.

called either a cabinet or a bookcase. The chief function of a room divider is to define the limits of a certain area in a room, such as a dining or a study area, and of course to provide storage and shelving.

Special Storage Pieces

Although most storage problems can be solved by the average storage cabinet or chest, there are many special-purpose pieces that may fit some of your needs better than flexible storage units. Such pieces might include a modern desk—vanity-shelf connected by two chests or cabinets, or a compartmented storage case to accommodate both a man's and a woman's small articles of clothing. Or, you might need a special cabinet designed to hold a television set and a hi-fi record player.

Storage Headboards

Not too many years ago, every bed had a headboard and a footboard. Later, the footboard was eliminated and just the headboard was retained. Then modern designers decided that if the headboard was to remain, it might as well be made useful, so a new "storage headboard" was developed to hold such articles as a radio, books, magazines, and, in some cases, an extra blanket. Gradually, other innovations have been added, such as side cabinets or shelves (as part of the storage headboard) to provide a surface for a breakfast tray, a telephone, or for writing; also back rests that can be tilted for reading comfort and adjustable reading lights have been included. In a small bedroom a storage headboard is a useful space-saving device, especially if it has attached cabinets or shelves.

Although there are many storage headboards imitating traditional and provincial styles, most of them have a clumsy, artificial appearance. The best designs are modern, but even some of these are clumsy and badly scaled. So if you want a storage headboard, be sure that it has simple lines and good proportions.

▶

Built-in drawers, shelves for bath and bedroom linens take one wall of the dressing room—bathroom. Top section is lined with quilted plastic. Drawers below are for table linens and kitchen towels.

Closets

One of the problems constantly faced in the small modern house or apartment is inadequate closet space. It is easy enough to plan good closet space when you build, but if you move into a new house or apartment, it is likely to have only one closet in each bedroom. If you haven't room or can't build another closet in your bedroom, the problem is to make one closet a convenient place to keep everything.

When a closet is used by two people, it is best to install some kind of division, such as a curtain or a plywood panel, so that each person has his own area for his clothing. It is best to have shoe racks that will hold at least six pairs of shoes for each person.

If your closet is large enough, you can use a storage piece at one side—either with shoe shelves below and shelves above to hold hats and handbags, or with shoe shelves below and shallow trays above for small articles of clothing.

Above the rods, put a shelf for hatboxes, out-of-season articles, and luggage. The inside of the door is a good place for a necktie rod or for shoe racks if there isn't room inside, and there may be room for a clothes brush. Or, you might hang a full-length mirror inside the door.

One way of gaining storage space in a bedroom with only one small closet is to build in wardrobelike closets. For instance, two such wardrobes might be built in on the wall spaces on either side of a window, and the entire wall space above the window and wardrobes could be filled in with small cupboards. You could enclose the wardrobes and cupboards with shuttered doors or with hinged or sliding doors painted the color of the walls. A built-in dressing table or a vanity could be placed against the wall space under the window.

A relatively inexpensive way of adding closet and storage space is to buy unpainted, prefabricated closets. They are available in widths from 2 to 6 feet and are equipped with rods, shelves, and drawers.

The narrow widths usually have hinged doors, while the wider ones have sliding doors. Prefabricated closets can have a built-in look if they are painted to harmonize with the room, or they can be covered with wallpaper to match the paper on the walls. Another way to create a dressing table niche in a bedroom, if you have wall space, is

▼ *In this dressing room for a man, prefabricated closet units have a built-in look. Storage boxes and chests are covered in brown quilted chintz and are arranged so everything is easy of access. Door at left slides back to reveal full-length hanging space.*

Careful study of the individual requirements of one ▲
man for stowing his gear evolved this system of
compartments, easily kept neat, behind a wall front
of handsomely grained wood paneling.

254

▼ *Compact and complete, a man's closet doubles as his dressing room, equipped with chest of drawers, hanging space, and shoe shelves. It's well lighted, has mirror-faced door and sleek, easy-to-clean vinyl floor.*

to place two prefabricated closets about thirty inches apart and connect them with a dressing table shelf (see illustrations, pages 91, 92). Also, a wide prefabricated closet makes a good room divider in a bedroom occupied by two children. Or you can use two such closets, set at right angles to each other, in a corner arrangement.

The ideal closet and storage arrangement for two people is one that is compartmented for each person with a double hanging space for clothing and with shelves or roomy trays for the smaller articles of clothing, racks for shoes, and shelves or cubicles for hats, handbags, and out-of-season articles. This type of compartmented closet can have double or sliding doors finished in wood paneling or painted or papered to harmonize with the room.

A separate dressing room or dressing-bathroom is often an ideal place for either built-in or prefabricated closets, because it may have more wall space than the bedroom.

Don't neglect the inside of your closets. You can make them as pretty as any other part of the room by painting them a gay contrasting color or wallpapering the inside with a gay pattern. You can also buy attractive, ready-made, dust-proof garment bags with either matching or contrasting boxes—to store hats, sweaters, and other articles—shoe bags, and hangers. There is a wide variety of ready-made closet accessories ranging from gaily patterned chintz or quilted chintz to attractive plastic fabrics.

Special Closets

Today almost every house needs special storage for household articles and for things that the different members of a family collect, including articles for such outdoor activities as games, picnics, barbecues, fishing, skiing, and so on.

In the old days, the attic was the catch-all for odds and ends and the bulky things used for sports and outdoor activities. Most new houses don't have attics, or if there is an attic, it may have been turned into a room that is used by one or more members of the family. So, storage space for all the sports equipment that keeps expanding each year is a problem.

The most practical solution is a sizable storage closet, conveniently located for every member of your family. The family room in the basement or the back hall might be a good place for a roomy closet. It can be either a built-in closet or a sizable prefabricated closet, and it should be attractive as well as functional. Pegboard or cork in a

▲ *This closet, shared by all the members of a sports-minded family, holds everyone's equipment and clothing. It's completely lined with peg-board. Hooks and holders in various groupings hold game and picnic gear, rainwear, and caps. An adjustable metal "tree" adds hanging space.*

bright color makes a practical wall covering for the inside because hooks and wire holders can be arranged in different groupings at different heights to hold such articles as tennis rackets, fishing tackle, picnic and barbecue equipment, hats, boots, and so on. For hanging sport jackets and coats, install either an adjustable metal tree, or sliding rods that can be pulled out into the room (see illustration, page 257).

To be practical, a linen closet for the average small house or apartment should be wide and shallow, rather than narrow and deep, but no inches should be wasted on doorjambs. Measure each stack of sheets and towels and be sure that the shelves will hold them. Another important linen-closet detail is storage for blankets, pillows, and comforters. Usually they are stuffed on an upper shelf where they gather

With doors closed, these closets in a commodious dressing room make a solid wall of mirrors. Divided for various hanging lengths, the space also affords five roomy drawers.

258

◄

Built-in closets, on either side of windows, form a recess in this bedroom for a built-in dressing table with mirrored top and storage space below.

dust and creases. The best solution is to put them on the lowest shelf that provides enough height, not necessarily depth; if they are not put into boxes, they will be easier to stack if the shelf is compartmented.

Although the linen closet is usually attractive by nature because of its colored sheets, towels, blankets, and other articles for the bedroom and bath, lining it with a quilted plastic fabric and adding a pretty edging on the shelves is a good incentive for keeping it neat and tidy.

In any event, the only way to make each closet practical and comfortable is to measure what you want to put in it and fit everything in to the best advantage, exactly as you would pack a bag.

As you study the illustrations, notice that each one demonstrates how storage space can be used advantageously, and how shelves, drawers, and closet accessories can help make the most of feet and inches.

▲

Compact wood-paneled storage wall, in modern dining room, provides space for dining-table appointments, and for sink and built-in radio phonograph.

▼

An impressive, well-designed built-in wall arrangement in this family room provides space for cooking, storage, TV set, even bookshelves.

▲ *A handsome arrangement of ceiling-to-floor wall cupboards done in provincial style with louvered doors at top does double duty as a pass-through to the kitchen in the section shown above. Counter serves as a buffet, also holds the television set. Spacious shelves above are for books.*

261

13 Accessories

A room may be decorated in the best of taste, with well-designed furniture, beautiful floor coverings, curtains, and upholstery, and have a harmonious color scheme, but it cannot and never will show individuality or real interest unless it is furnished with the kind of tasteful accessories that reflect the personality of those who live in it. A hotel room, for example, may be nicely furnished and completed with attractive accessories, but it will always seem impersonal or flat to those who occupy it because it fails to reflect a personal touch.

An accessory is a decorative aid. It may be a purely decorative object, such as a lovely ceramic figure or a handsome wood carving, or it may be essentially utilitarian, such as a lamp or an ashtray. Whatever it is, any accessory you choose should not only have beauty of form and color and harmonize with your furnishings and other accessories, but should also give a distinctive touch to the room and reflect your tastes and personality. Since accessories are such important decorative aids, you would be wise to shop for them cautiously and be certain that the kind of objects you are looking for will add distinction to your furnishings.

◀

An air of importance is given this low sideboard by the use of sizable accessories, as tall vase, tray of decanters, and elegant barometer.

If you are in doubt about your taste, study these illustrations; they will help you choose accessories for any room in your home. As you acquire knowledge through study and observation, you will soon learn to recognize with increasing surety the difference between the tasteful and the commonplace. For example, you will see innumerable mass-produced articles, such as trite china figurines or insipid ashtrays and other meaningless trivia. Though they are often made of fairly good materials and have reasonably good proportions, they are of such commonplace, standardized, and tiresome design that they lack distinction or aesthetic appeal, and so fall short of the requirements of good taste.

Good taste is based on trained judgment—that is, the ability to distinguish between the well-designed, distinctive, and aesthetically satisfying, and the undistinguished, commonplace, or even downright ugly. Thus, a connoisseur or expert is trained through study and observation to discriminate between qualities, and learns to have an appreciation of what is best.

Some people have excellent taste but lack imagination enough to put it to work. For example, even rooms that are quite tastefully decorated can fail in individuality if no imagination is applied to the selection of the accessories. The person whose taste is sure and who shows imagination resorts to neither safe, conventional accessories, nor bizarre or vulgar ones. He tries to find objects that are as suitable as they are unique and distinctive.

When you choose accessories for any room in your home, be sure that the objects are appropriate for the places you put them and the way they are to be used, and that they are compatible with your other furnishings. For instance, an elaborate eighteenth-century Venetian chandelier in a room decorated with simple, informal provincial furnishings, would be neither suitable nor compatible. Also, to avoid a cluttered effect, be sure to use restraint in the placement and arrangement of accessories. Always consider the area you are decorating, be it a mantel, a table, or any other space, as a minor composition. On your coffee table, for example, you will need one or two sizable ashtrays, an attractive cigarette box (avoid prosaic ashtray and cigarette box sets), either a bowl of flowers or fruit or a "conversation piece"—such as a sculpture piece or ceramic figure—and a few current magazines or other accouterments that will make the table attractive and useful.

▲ *A few unique and important accessories, such as the large sculptured head, abstract painting, tall covered glass jar and modern lanternlike hanging lights, skillfully arranged, make a dramatic focal point at one end of this contemporary living room.*

▼ *Accessories for a formal, traditional room, like the ones shown in this still life, although of different periods and of different materials, still have the same character and the same feeling of elegance.*

▶

Brass candlesticks, pewter covered dish, and earthenware objects mixed with simple white milk glass covered "hen" dish, plate, and candlestick, would add decorative interest to a provincial dining room, as shown in still life.

▲ *Simple contemporary accessories of metal and wood combine pleasantly with countrified objects of pewter, glass, earthenware, and woven reed, as pictured in this still life.*

▲ *A grouping of old maps, old prints, and montage of pistols, hung above this simple table-desk, set the theme for a man's den. Lamp made from an old wooden candlestick, brass tobacco container, and mug used for pencils complete the rugged feeling.*

You can often give a room particular distinction by using a discriminating combination of old and new accessories. Don't be afraid to mix the really fine antique objects that can provide a charming personal touch with well-designed modern accessories. But be sure that they are harmonious with your other furnishings and suitable for the places you are going to put them.

Above all, the accessories you choose must have the intrinsic qualities of good scale and proportion, as well as beauty of shape and color. Accessories need not be expensive, but they must be chosen with great care. There is a fairly good selection of inexpensive accessories available, such as opaline glass in lovely colors, relatively inexpensive lamps, good prints and reproductions of paintings, and handsome oriental objects.

Since scale and proportion are so important in the decoration of a room, you should have an understanding of these terms. *Scale* refers to the relation of the size of an object to other objects, while *proportion* refers to the relationship of each part of an object to every other part. For example, if a lampshade is too high and too wide for the base, it is out of proportion to its base. And even if the lampshade is the right size for the base, the lamp as a whole might be too small or too large in scale for the table it is placed on. It is not always necessary that all details in a room be in correct scale for the size of the room itself (sometimes overscaling is very effective), but they should be in proper relationship or proportion to each other.

Collections

A collection of unusual and interesting objects should be displayed together against the best background you can give them. Make your collection a focal point in the room, by arranging it in an attractive grouping on well-lighted shelves, on a wall, in a cupboard, or in a glass-topped table. Such collector's items as old embroideries and

Elegant accessories add charm and individuality to this formal traditional living room. The handsome lamp, graceful tea set, and flowers in lace-work ceramic bowl mingle pleasantly with satin-covered sofa and Louis XVI cane-back chair and sofa-table.

needlepoint can make a charming decorative arrangement over a mantel or on the wall above a chest. A collection too might provide the accent color in a room; for example, you could use cerulean-blue Bristol glass displayed on a chest or in a cupboard and repeat the same shade in small chairs and pillows. In kitchens, too, collections of such objects as copper kettles and molds, trivets, and other articles commonly used in the kitchen can be displayed to advantage. More than almost any other accessory, interesting collections tastefully arrayed give a personal touch that will never fail to give pleasure.

Lamps

Lamps—although some architects and designers consider them obsolete—are still indispensable because they give a room a cozy, personal feeling never achieved with built-in illumination alone. Among kinds of lamps available are the portable variety for tables and desks, standing floor lamps, and pulley lights.

When you choose a lamp, be sure that it is the right scale for the objects that will be used around it. It should provide good reading light, and should not shine directly into the eyes of the people seated nearby. If you fit your lamps with indirect reflectors the glare will be reduced.

Most living rooms and bedrooms need at least five lamps, and their sizes and general character should harmonize with each other and with the other furnishings. For example, in a provincial living room, there might be a pair of brass lamps and a pair of wooden lamps made from old mortars and pestles, and the fifth might be a painted tole lamp.

Portable lamps or pulley wall lamps are generally best for desks and tables that are used for work and reading, but floor lamps are a useful alternative, especially near a drop-leaf desk or a piano. Any lamp with an opaque shade can be used for viewing television to avoid eyestrain caused by TV watching in a completely darkened room.

Shades should be the right size for the bases, simply shaped, and of such simple materials as silk, linen, or paper. It is generally best to use a neutral color or off-white, and the inside of all shades should be white for efficient light reflection.

▶

An antique screen, with delicate pierced design, makes a distinctive wall decoration in back of sofa and combines pleasantly with contemporary furniture and accessories.

270

Certain types of lamps have affinity for certain kinds of rooms, but you need not always choose lamps of the same period. For example a pair of simple modern wood bases would combine well with a pair of old tea-cannister bases, and a fifth lamp might be an old French tole student's lamp. Or, in a rather stark modern room warmth and distinction would be given by using a pair of old French brass oil lamps and a pair of old carved wood bases.

Unusual accessories, like the antique mortar and pestles, old canisters, and toy cannon, not only add decorative interest to grouping on this low modern chest, but also have added merit of starting conversation.

An interesting grouping of delicate Chinese paintings, with flat gilt frames, a decorative oriental lattice-work screen, and lovely blanc de chine figurines give an elegant touch to contemporary furniture of Chinese inspiration.

An important Chinese painting, an old lacquered box, and a pair of ceramic birds give this modern room, with Chinese-inspired contemporary furniture and brass tree-lamp, great distinction.

273

An individual and interesting background for a collection of carved birds is the whitewashed raised brick fireplace in this modern living room.

Mantel Decoration

Because the fireplace is one of the most important focal points in a room, the decorative treatment should be carefully planned. Above all, don't clutter up the mantel shelf with small objects or be satisfied with a conventional arrangement of a bowl in the center with a candlestick on each side. If you already have a matching set, try placing the two candlesticks side-by-side at one end of the mantel shelf and the bowl, filled with greens, at the other; add to this a sizable picture or a grouping of pictures hung on the wall over the mantel. Even a conventional arrangement of a pair of objects can be pleasing and interesting if you combine unusual objects. You might use a pair of urns filled with flowers or greens, with a beautiful old clock in the center; or a pair of candlesticks, combined with a ceramic epargne filled with fruit and flowers; or a pair of covered Chinese vases, with a grouping of small potted plants in a decorative oval container in the center of the mantel shelf.

Aside from the asymmetrical arrangement of decorative objects (with two or more objects on one side of the mantel shelf, balanced by a single weighty object on the other side) you might use rows of such similar objects as well-scaled pitchers or apothecary jars, candlesticks, or Chinese clay figures. If the mantel is small, one important decorative object placed in the center may be sufficient; you might use a large tureen filled with greens, an interesting wood carving, or a long, boat-shaped dish filled with fruit or foliage.

If your fireplace has no mantel shelf, look for objects that will give a dramatic effect when placed against the chimney breast. You could select, for example an important painting, a collection of unusual prints, a Chinese scroll, an old carved figure, an old weather vane, or a fragment of an old carving.

Your fire tongs, andirons, and fender should be sturdy and in proper scale to the fireplace. If you want to be safe, use brass fire accessories, but keep them bright and shiny.

▼ *A collection of eagles, mostly carved ones, gives an individual decorative touch to this simple contemporary bedroom.*

A spot of daring will make for individuality: To wit, copper molds become striking ornaments over copper-toned fireplace and planter, group well with black obelisks and pinky-grays of the fish picture. Couch cover reflects them, too.

▼

Hobbies, special interests may, any of them, provide a theme for accessories. For example, a love of the sea inspired the fresh modern grouping of shells, ceramic and metal fish on shelves below.

No part of decorating is more fun than choosing accessories for any room in your home. Treasured possessions, like the ones pictured in the still life here, contribute so much in charm, color, and character to any decorating scheme. ▶

A collection of Bristol-blue glass, skillfully grouped on a Regency chest against off-white walls, sets the color scheme for this room. The background of the picture grouping, a leather chair, and other touches match it exactly.

This charming desk arrangement has great distinction because the accessories and picture grouping, of different periods and materials, are completely harmonious.

Pictures

Well-chosen and interesting pictures, like a collection of unusual hobby objects, contribute more to the decorative theme and personal touch in a room than most other accessories. Your selection of pictures is also one of the most revealing clues to your taste. And you can find all kinds of worthwhile art in things you never thought of before. To give a few examples, a collection of old prints (such as old theatrical prints), good reproductions of modern paintings combined with line drawings, a collection of butterflies framed in shadow boxes, old maps, a handsome poster (like those of Toulouse-Lautrec or E. McKnight Kauffer), or an old oriental screen hung flat on the wall can be used to aesthetic advantage.

Whatever you do, avoid overfamiliar paintings, or prosaic flower prints. Some reproductions of good paintings are too small to be hung singly and should be used in groups; on the other hand, distinctive reproductions that are the same size as the original painting are also available, and these create an impressive effect even when hung alone. Elaborate frames, unless they are antiques, are less effective than simple styles, and all frames should harmonize with one another. However, you need not use matching frames. Modern pictures and posters are often mounted or stretched on thin strip moldings painted to match the walls.

Although there is no set rule for hanging pictures, it is generally best if they are logically related to a piece of furniture, such as a chest or a sofa, or to an architectural feature, such as a mantel. A trend today is to hang a large picture group from the ceiling to a very low level. Wall clocks, barometers, and fragments of wood or stone carving combine well with a grouping of pictures. Also, a picture not hung may be part of a decorative arrangement on a chest, desk, or table, with a bowl of flowers and a candelabra.

Bookshelves

Decorative objects can be interspersed among books on shelves to provide an attractive display. But beautifully bound volumes may not need added accessories because they themselves contribute color, pattern, and interest to any room. Decorative objects that can be pleasingly combined with books, might include a collection of such hobby objects as old white ironstone or unusual shells, an assortment of accessories from many periods, or both small paintings and plants.

▲ *A collection of butterflies in shadow boxes, appropriately displayed on the bookshelves below with plants, books, and other decorative objects, makes a point of interest in the room.*

Screens

Today screens have become an important accessory in many rooms because they can be at once decorative and thoroughly useful. One lovely screen can become the focal point in a room if there is no fireplace; or it can be used to define an area, such as a dining area in a living room; or to define an entry way to a living room; or a pair of tall narrow screens can be used to frame a window.

For a modest price you can make your own screens. A very inexpensive screen can be constructed of simple machine-guard metal, or translucent plastic attached to a wood frame. Or, you can make your own screen by attaching cloth to a frame or by covering a wallboard screen with fabric or unusual wallpaper.

Minor Accessories

Ashtrays should be easily accessible and they should be sizable, because very small ashtrays soon fill up with ashes which spill onto the table. Frankly, good-looking ashtrays are hard to find, although some of domestic or imported glass and some of modern ceramics are attractive. But with a little imagination and ingenuity you can create ashtrays out of many other things—old ceramic or brass plates, or leaf-shaped and shell-shaped dishes.

A vase of flowers or greens, growing plants, and bowls of fruit and nuts lend warmth and a personal touch to even a hotel room. Since cut flowers are expensive, if you don't have a flower garden you may prefer to use greens, such as rhododendron leaves, laurel, magnolia, or pine. They will last a long time. Artificial flowers and fruit are also becoming popular, but if they are not arranged with imagination and style, they look cheap and ugly. However, sometimes a few artificial flowers added to natural leaves can fool the eye.

Clear glass vases are, generally, best for flowers and greens, but small bouquets of flowers make a charming decorative note in a low silver, old ceramic, or colored opaline bowl. Potted plants are also attractive when they are grouped together—for instance, in wire stands, in a basket on a table, or in a trough or stand in the window—or arranged in a row on a mantel.

▶

A discriminating combination of sculpture, plants, books, and antique objects, tastefully arranged on modern hanging shelves, provides a charming personal touch to this room.

14 How to Buy

When you go out to shop for furnishings for your home, you will find a wealth of merchandise, a multitude of styles, materials, colors, and qualities available. This impressive variety gives you ample opportunity to suit your own personal tastes, but it can also be confusing. For this reason we give some information in this chapter which will help you to know what to look for in terms of appropriateness and quality.

A few general bits of advice are: don't begin to shop until you have a carefully thought-out plan; go slowly—don't feel you have to do the whole job at once; and, above all, don't be swayed by what the mythical "they" are supposed to be buying or doing. Take measurements or, if possible, a scaled floor plan of the room with you when you shop. If you are not experienced with color, try to get large samples of wallpaper and fabrics even if you have to buy them; don't work from snippets, as colors may look different in small samples from the way they would look in a large area. And of course, shop in a reputable store or through a decorator who will stand behind the merchandise you purchase. Sometimes it is fun to ferret out what you think is a bargain at a mill-end or a cut-rate outlet, but beware: you do so at your own risk.

Learn what trade expressions do and do not mean. Many of these are used quite loosely in stores and their advertising; for example, "early American" may embrace anything from seventeenth- and eighteenth-century maple and pine, to nineteenth-century Hitch-cock chairs and Pennsylvania Dutch. Or you may be puzzled by the varying meanings for which the term "traditional" is used: it is sometimes a synonym for American or English eighteenth-century furniture in all its variations, but it may include nineteenth-century styles—French, English, and American, antiques or reproductions, both good and bad. In fact, sometimes people use the word to cover all styles before modern. And those words "modern" and "contemporary," which are often used interchangeably, can be confusing *too. Strictly speaking, "contemporary" means present-day styles; "modern" can have the same meaning, but often it is used to describe the break with tradition which took place in the 1920's and the '30's and the designs it inspired.*

WHEN YOU BUY FURNITURE

Generally speaking you know the style you want, the number and kind of pieces you need, and the dimensions of the room you will be working with. But one of the first traps for the unwary furniture shopper is the matched set of furniture for one flat price. It often seems like a good buy, but even where the quality is of the very best, the monotony of matching woods can make your room seem commonplace. Nowadays nearly all stores sell furniture from "open stock," which means you can choose only as many matching pieces from one group as you need and want. You'll often find it effective to use one piece in a wood different from the rest of the furniture: for example, a pine breakfront in a room with mahogany, or a lacquered or painted piece of furniture with natural wood. Don't be afraid to mix furniture styles; only remember that they should be appropriate together in terms of formality or informality.

▲ *This handsome contemporary storage cabinet has beauty of grain and finish. The wooden drawer pulls add a decorative note to an otherwise plain surface.*

WHAT TO LOOK FOR IN CABINETWORK

The bulk of American-made furniture is well constructed; methods, materials, and finishing techniques have been developed that guarantee the purchaser a quality product.

The surfaces should have beauty of color, grain, and finish. Make sure that the veneers have been expertly matched and that the finishing operations have been performed with care. If correctly finished, the piece should have uniformity of color, and the surfaces should be smooth—free of tool marks, raised grain, scratches, or dents. Moldings, if present, should be crisp and clean looking, and the joints at the corners should be carefully matched and mitered. Notice particularly the back of such pieces as cabinets and chests. The back panel should be carefully screwed and glued in place, finished, and rubbed.

Then examine the joints on the inside. They must be smooth, tight, and perfectly fitted; no glue should be visible. Any gaps between joints are an indication of poor workmanship. Make sure there are no nails, as nails are never used in good furniture.

Here is a list of the best-known joints. They have been used for centuries with almost no change in design.

Plain butt: The simplest type of joint but unsuitable where strain might be set up in the joint.

Mortise and tenon: One of the oldest joints used in furniture construction. Pegs and dowels are used for reinforcement at times, and sometimes screws are similarly used. They are usually countersunk and covered with a wooden plug for the sake of appearance.

Corner joints: The simplest is a rabbeted (grooved) joint; the best is the locked joint. In addition, all large furniture and chairs should be reinforced with well-fitted corner blocks held in place by screws.

Dovetail joints: These right-angle joints are a sign of the best workmanship. They resist strain in any direction.

The factory machines that do the joinery for the finest furniture must be of the highest degree of precision, because the slightest variation in boring or shaping any of the points of contact (of two pieces that are to be fitted together) will result in a weak joint.

Drawers *reveal the quality of a piece of furniture more quickly than any other part. The best construction will always show dovetail joints at the front and back, while less expensive pieces are dovetailed in front and the back is slipped into a groove.*

Look at the underside of the drawer. It should be strengthened at each corner with corner block, and the bottom panel—at least ¼ inch thick—should be grooved into the sides and front panel.

Test the drawers to see that they slide easily and smoothly. The best type of drawer slide is either a center slide of well-seasoned wood, glued to the bottom of the drawer from front to back, or a metal slide. The side slide is the least expensive type of drawer slide. Notice, too, whether there are dust panels between the drawers; they are not essential, but if present they should be of hardwood. The insides of the drawers should be of veneer or solid hardwood; they should be lacquered, waxed, and smooth to the touch.

Tops of chests, cabinets, and tables should be attached with screws or dowels or with special metal clips. Glue, if used alone, is affected by shrinking or warping.

Legs should be made of one piece of wood.

Hardware, including handles, drawer pulls, and keyhole plates, is an important detail and should not be overlooked. Pay special attention to the design and workmanship, as hardware is the "jewelry" of a piece, and the wrong selection can detract from otherwise good furniture. Remember that well-designed hardware gives a piece of furniture a distinctive touch.

An easy rule to follow is, the simpler the piece of furniture, the plainer the design of the hardware. The hardware should not only be the right proportion for the scale of the furniture, but it should also be the right design for the style involved. It might be a good idea for you to acquaint yourself with the different types of hardware, especially the designs of the eighteenth century and the simple contemporary designs (some are quite oriental in feeling). You'll find the older style of hardware on antiques in museums or antique shops, and on the best reproductions, and examples of traditional and contemporary designs in catalogs in the better hardware stores.

Woods. For fine furniture, a wood should be hard enough to resist denting, strong enough to provide rigidity, distinctive enough in pattern or grain to be beautiful, and as lightweight as possible.

Some woods have desirable physical properties for the manufacture of furniture, such as strength or workability, but lack such decorative features as beauty of color and distinctive grain or pattern, while other woods are valued for their intrinsic beauty.

Definite rules were set up by the Federal Trade Commission (in 1925) for describing wood furniture, whether on tags, in advertising copy, or in catalogs. All wood descriptions apply only to exposed surfaces. (These rules do not apply to antique furniture.) Machine-made furniture is labeled according to the species of wood or woods for the exposed surfaces, and the labels specify whether a wood is solid, veneer, or a combination of solid and veneer. Woods stained to resemble hardwoods have such labels as "Mahogany Finish" or "Walnut Finish." The labeling relates only to the finish, not to the wood itself, which may be birch, maple, red gum, or some other.

SOLID WOODS VS. VENEER

Many people are confused by these terms, and have an idea that veneered furniture is somehow inferior and that there is a special virtue in something described as "solid." Actually much fine furniture is veneered; and both veneered and solid wood pieces can be either good or bad, depending on other factors.

The dictionary defines "veneer" as a thin sheet of choice wood glued or bonded to another wood, usually less choice. In cabinetwork this technique makes possible the beautiful matched markings in the grain that you see in much traditional and modern furniture.

▲ *Beautifully grained wood, enhanced by graceful brass hardware, gives this spacious contemporary storage chest great distinction.*

290

Cutting and slicing different logs to achieve the desired effect is an art in itself. In fine furniture the framework and base to which this outer layer is attached should be of sturdy hardwood, often the same variety of wood (mahogany, walnut, oak, maple, for example) as the outer layer. However many decorative woods are too soft to be used structurally, and are only suitable for veneers and inlays.

In pieces of furniture labeled solid mahogany, maple, pine, or walnut, you will find that the exposed surfaces, such as the doors, tops, and drawer fronts are made from solid pieces of wood, as are the framing and supporting structure. Naturally this gives you a sturdy piece of furniture if it is well made, but the refinements of design and enhancement of the wood patterns are usually sacrificed. Consequently the plainer, less formal styles (such as early American maple and pine, and American Colonial mahogany and walnut pieces) are better suited to solid constructions, though these also are occasionally veneered.

Much of the contemporary-styled furniture nowadays, with its smooth expanses of beautifully marked wood surfaces, is made of modern veneered plywood. Plywood *is a term most of us think of as describing a building material, but it means the bonding of thin sheets or plies together with the grain running in alternate directions. This ancient technique, now accomplished by machinery with synthetic resins, produces a panel many times stronger than a solid plank of the same thickness. Fine veneers may be bonded to the outer surfaces of the panels; quality furniture usually has five to seven layers in the core, while less expensive varieties may have only three.*

MOLDED PLYWOOD

The modern technique of laminating plywood under heat and pressure makes it possible to bend and shape it to fit a mold. Thus you will see chairs with the whole seat, arms, and back molded out of one piece, and sometimes a complete table or a specially shaped top.

Finishing. *The primary function of a finish is to protect and preserve the wood surface from dirt, liquids, and marring, and to provide an outer coat that can be easily cleaned. The second function of a finish is to enhance the beauty of the furniture. Often the finish determines the difference in price of two similar pieces of furniture. The finest furniture is finished by hand, which may involve as many as fifteen or more processes. Moderately priced furniture may be hand-finished with fewer processes, or a combination of machine and hand finishes may be used. Keep this in mind: usually the cheapest finish is also the shiniest, while the finest finish has a soft, mellow gleam from much rubbing rather than the high gloss of shellac.*

The term finish *refers to other treatments besides those that reveal the natural grain or figure of wood. Special finishes may include fine lacquering, stippling, and crackling, as well as effects simulating marbles, porphyry, tortoise shell, lapis lazuli, and many others.*

Staining, an important part of finishing, is used to change the color or tone of the wood. Woods may be either stained with a pigment solution or bleached to remove the color.

UPHOLSTERED FURNITURE

It is a little more difficult to appraise upholstered furniture than any other home-furnishings article. The chief reason is, of course, that so much of the important structure is hidden. Thus it is important to buy only from the most reputable houses.

When you shop for upholstered pieces, remember first of all that bulk is not a guarantee of comfort or quality; look rather for pieces that are of the right size and shape for your particular purpose. Even though all stores carry three-piece sets and these are often well made, the trend is away from such matched sets. Another thing to remember: simple lines stay in style much longer and will harmonize well with many different styles of rooms.

▲ *This graceful and well-constructed contemporary armchair may be combined with either modern or traditional furniture. Ottoman can be used for extra seating.*

Well-made upholstered pieces are a prime investment in furnishing your home; you expect them to wear for years, and though good pieces are not cheap, you should buy the best you can afford. If a good sofa is out of reach of your beginning budget, put your money into a good lounge chair (you'll need one anyway) and several occasional chairs. Or you can buy one or two parts of a sectional sofa (making sure of course that the store will continue selling the group until you are ready to purchase the other sections in the next year or so). If you like to entertain house guests, you may want to consider a folding sofa bed. Or, a simple box spring, and mattress, slipcovered, with neatly tailored cushions, makes a good dual-purpose sitting and sleeping arrangement.

In choosing upholstery fabrics, try to look at them in both artificial light and daylight. If you can, borrow swatches to look at in your home; otherwise, take samples of your wall and carpet colors with you. Don't feel you are confined to tough and practical materials. There are many durable upholstery fabrics available today that are soft to the hand, easy to care for, comfortable to sit on, and beautiful as well. Some of the fabrics you might like are heavy cottons (including a new cotton velvet that doesn't shade), quiltlike fabrics that wear for many years, interesting textured weaves damasks made of many long-wearing fibers, nylon velvets, and some handsome plastic fabrics. Some plastic fabrics have woven effects; others simulate leather.

Slipcovers are now used all year and are suitable for all styles of formal or informal furniture. Even on new muslin-covered furniture, you will find that slipcovers are easier to maintain than upholstery because they can be removed for cleaning or laundering.

Slipcovers can be made of almost any kind of closely woven material, from costly damasks and antique satins to velveteen, quilted chintz, cottons, linens, and combinations of fibers of all kinds.

Here are a few tips about choosing upholstery fabrics or slip-covers.

1. In small or medium-sized living rooms, it is a good idea to have the color of your large upholstered pieces, particularly the sofa, relate to the color of the walls or floor covering, not contrast with them.

2. If your room is a large one, you might use a bright contrasting color on a sofa or a pair of chairs.

3. Slipcovering or upholstering all large pieces in one important bold or bright pattern helps to unify a large room, especially if it is sparsely furnished otherwise.

▲ *The striking, widely-spaced design on the smartly tailored slipcover in no way competes with the delicate, over-all wallpaper pattern.*

WHAT ABOUT REUPHOLSTERING?

Reupholstering is worthwhile only if the sofa and chairs have good, timeless, simple designs, or if the frames are antiques or fine carving. Reupholstering does not mean merely removing the old cover and recovering the piece with a new fabric. If it is in bad repair, a good upholsterer strips the piece all the way down to its wooden frame. He strengthens the frame if necessary, and also replaces the webbing, reties the old springs (if they haven't lost their resiliency) or replaces them with new ones, and supplies new filling for seats, arms, back, and cushions; all of this is before he even begins to put on a new fabric. To have a fine piece of furniture well reupholstered is a good investment, as it usually costs less than buying equally good pieces at today's prices. It is a good idea, before you give an order to have anything reupholstered, to do a little comparison shopping. You will find that prices for new well-designed and well-made upholstered furniture have more than doubled during the last ten years. After looking at new furniture, you may discover that your old pieces look more cumbersome and commonplace than you thought they did. In this case, it would be wise to dispose of them and buy new upholstered furniture, even if you can buy only one piece at a time.

DRAPERY FABRICS AND CURTAINS

Before you embark on your shopping tour for drapery fabrics (if you are making the draperies yourself) measure your windows carefully. Measure windows from the top of the rod to the sill or to the floor (depending on whether the draperies are to be sill length or floor length) and from the outer edge of the window frame on one side to the outer edge on the other side. Draperies that are to be drawn across the windows should be one and a half to two times the width of the window, to allow for fullness. Be sure to measure each window, even if they appear to be all the same size.

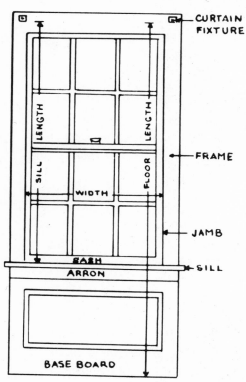

Decide in advance exactly what your room needs. If you are buying fabric for replacement draperies, take swatches of the slip-cover and other materials you already have in the room and of your carpet with you when you go shopping. Bring home samples of all of the fabrics you like and try them in the room by both daylight and artificial light. Don't buy a single piece of fabric until you have made all your selections and have tried the samples at home.

If you are shopping for a pattern, be sure that it is right for the room, this is especially important if you have a patterned rug, such as an Oriental carpet with a prominent design. In such a room, solid colors are usually best, but you can use a stripe or perhaps a small allover pattern, if the windows are not very large. If you are combining two printed fabrics in one room, be sure there is a marked difference in scale—that is, that one pattern is considerably larger than the other; two different patterns the same size would compete with each other. If you have a large picture window, bear in mind that bold-print draperies drawn across the window may dwarf the rest of the room. If your room is sparsely furnished, one important pattern for draperies, repeated on a slipcover for a sofa or on slipcovers for two lounge chairs, will help to give your room a "furnished" look. Use more fabric design if you intend to hang few pictures than if you plan to hang many.

There is also a wide variety of good-looking ready-made draperies, but be sure to take one pair home to try out before you buy draperies for all the windows.

▲ *A neat over-all design, repeated in draperies and ottoman, adds pattern to this modern room. The colors in the design are picked up in upholstery and pillows.*

▲ *Simple tailored draperies with pinch-pleated tops, hung from ceiling to floor on the window wall, act as a foil for the modern furniture and help to give added height to this contemporary living room.*

Curtains may be roughly divided into two groups: glass curtains and casement curtains. Sheer curtains are most often used as glass curtains to eliminate glare and to soften the lines of the windows, though some glass curtains (such as embroidered organdies and ruffled curtains) are often used in place of heavy draperies. On the other hand, casement curtains are usually made of semisheer, translucent material, and are used in place of heavier drapery fabrics. Sometimes casement curtains are used as draw curtains under draperies to replace glass curtains.

In choosing drapery and curtain fabrics you must shop carefully and wisely because of the variety of materials available. Many of the fabrics, for example, serve a specific purpose, and you will want to decide which of the natural or man-made fibers are best for your own window treatments. For drapery fabrics it is wise to check for guarantee against fading, to find out whether the material can be laundered or must be cleaned, and to investigate other pertinent factors.

FLOOR COVERINGS

A greater advance in new materials and techniques for manufacturing carpeting has been made in the last ten years than in the previous ten centuries. Today, we have not only the traditional woven carpets and rugs, but also a new kind of carpeting made by machine tufting. This has placed carpets of excellent quality in beautiful colors and textures within reach of the consumer at much lower cost than conventional woven carpeting. Also many new carpet fibers are now in common use, such as rayon, nylon, Acrilan, blends of rayon and nylon, and other synthetic fibers.

Here are some of the facts you should know about carpet fibers.

Wool: The traditional fiber for carpets and still a favorite. Wool carpets, well constructed, will be serviceable for years. They have more resiliency than carpets made of other yarns.

Rayon: The use of rayon fibers developed especially for carpets is relatively new, and rayon carpets—particularly tufted ones—have revolutionized the carpet market by making available beautiful fashion-colored carpets at moderate prices. On the other hand, rayon carpets do not have as much crush resistance as wool, and cleaning is more difficult.

Cotton: The major advantages of cotton carpets or rugs are their relatively low price and the ease with which cotton can be dyed. Though cotton has good resistance to abrasion and will withstand hard wear, it will mat down and show crush marks, leaving an uneven shadowy texture. Cotton carpets are more difficult to keep clean than wool and some of the newer synthetic fibers, and the lighter shades require frequent professional plant cleaning, except for small scatter rugs which can go in the washer.

Nylon: Nylon carpeting has a thick, soft pile. Most stains can be washed off with warm sudsy water. The use of a detergent is recommended because soap, unless thoroughly rinsed, will leave a film and hasten resoiling. Nylon carpets and rugs are highly resistant to wear and will not show crushing as readily as cotton and rayon. Moths will not attack nylon and it is not affected by mildew. Because of the low moisture content of nylon, carpets made of it generate more static than those of cotton, rayon, or wool. Though nylon won't blaze up, carpets or rugs can be damaged by sparks, which will fuse the fibers. Nylon carpets and rugs are more expensive than rayon or cotton, but their initial cost should be weighed against the fact that they clean easily and will wear for years.

Saran: Saran carpeting has many of the properties of nylon. It is highly resistant to staining; even ink won't spot Saran carpets. It has good resistance to wear and crushing and is moderately priced. The color range of Saran carpets is more limited than rayon or cotton. Though they won't fade, the colors may darken slightly from exposure to sunlight.

Acrilan: A carpet of Acrilan is resilient, looks and feels like wool, and wears as well. It resists soil and is easy to clean. It is also moth- and mildewproof, is nonallergic, and has low static qualities and superior twist-retention.

Blends: Blends consist of combinations of two or more different fibers to achieve colors and properties not attainable by the use of a single fiber. For example, wool blended with rayon in a 50:50 ratio has many of the properties of both fibers; it is considerably less expensive than all-wool carpeting, can be made to wear as well, and is available in brighter colors than pure wool carpeting. A blend of 10 to 20 percent nylon with wool or rayon gives a carpet increased abrasion resistance. Remember, though, that the addition of less than 10 per cent of any fiber has little discernible effect on the carpet.

Re-used wool: Some excellent rugs are made of re-used wool. You send your old rug to the manufacturer as part of the purchase price, and he works it into an attractive, long-wearing, reversible rug for you. Such rugs have been found to be very satisfactory.

The very decided advantage of this vast array of different kinds of carpeting is that you are now able to buy exactly the carpet you need for a particular purpose. For example, a family with growing children can choose an extremely practical twist of mixed tweedy color; or, if more luxurious effects are desired, the selection is limitless.

The new and popular area rugs add a distinctive note to a handsome flooring, such as parquet wood flooring, rubber tile, cork, or vinyl tile floorings. Area rugs are quite different from small scatter rugs in that they are used primarily to unite furniture groupings, such as a fireplace or dining grouping. They are available in various sizes, shapes, textures, and designs. In an open-plan contemporary house, for example, where different areas in one room may be used for different activities (as in a living room with a dining area), rugs may divide activity zones. Generally, rectangular shapes are best because they can be shifted around so that they wear evenly, and they fit more conveniently into particular furniture groupings.

Finding a color and pattern that will blend harmoniously with your room is important, but the kind of service a carpet or rug will

299

give depends on such factors as the way it is made and the kind of fiber or combination of fibers used. Here are facts that you should know when you go shopping.

Pile: The pile on any carpet or rug is an important factor in determining wear resistance and appearance. The more yarns per square inch, or the denser the pile, the longer it will wear and the less it will crush or mat down. Especially with rayon and cotton carpets, be sure to notice whether the pile is short or long. For example, a short, twisted, cotton pile will show crushing less than a long-cut pile in solid colors. Often a short wool pile is more practical than a long pile for rooms that have heavy traffic; naturally, it is not as luxurious looking.

Backing: The backing is the material with which the pile is woven or to which it is tufted. It may be cotton canvas, duck, or jute. Backing also may mean a treatment given these materials, usually an application of some form of latex. Latex backing is used on nearly all tufted carpets to give extra body and cushioning and to help prevent skidding. Good latex backing will wear well, will not mar floors, and is not affected by radiant heating. Some tufted carpets now have a new type of cushiony rubber backing with built-in air pockets which prevents the pile from stretching or buckling and makes the carpet lie flat on the floor.

Colorfastness: It is important to know that your carpet color will not change or fade in sunlight or in cleaning. Wool usually has good colorfastness, but with cotton and rayon you are safer if there is a label which states that the yarns are vat-dyed; this process produces colors of great permanence. Of course, some colors and shades are more fugitive than others; vibrant, high-fashion colors tend to lose their brilliance and show soil faster than muted or neutral shades.

Many people are baffled and confused by descriptive terms like "Axminster," "Wilton," "velvet," "Brussels," "tufted," "chenille," and so on. Actually, these terms refer to the construction of the carpeting and different terms mean different ways in which the wool pile is woven in with the backing and filler material.

For instance, Axminster *can usually be identified by the heavy cross ridges on the back and by the fact that it will roll in only one direction—lengthwise. The tuft yarns forming the pile are all on the surface, and none are buried as in the case of a Wilton. Axminsters may be plain or woven in patterns.*

Wilton *carpeting has a rich, plushlike surface; the pile yarns are firmly woven with a back of cotton warp, weft, and stuffer yarns. None of the pile yarn will show through, and the rug is flexible enough to roll or fold across as well as longways.* Brussels *carpet*

▲ *The area rug in this distinctive contemporary living room adds a warm note to the polished hard flooring. It also helps to unite the grouping of furniture around the fireplace.*

is constructed on the same type of looms, with minor changes, as Wilton, but in Brussels the looped wool pile is uncut. Both types may be plain or patterned.

Velvet *carpeting is less expensive to manufacture than Wilton. Velvet is woven so that all of the wool yarn goes into the surface tufts and much of the carpet's body is supplied by the cotton warp and the jute stuffer yarns. This same weave with uncut looped pile is known as* tapestry *carpeting. Good quality velvet may wear better and be a better buy than poor quality Wilton.*

Chenille *carpet weaving involves two distinct processes. The first is to make the "chenille blanket" of wool, and cut it up into strips that are steamed and folded to form the chenille fur. These strips are then woven on another loom and form the pile surface of the carpet. Chenille makes a rich, luxurious floor-covering, and is usually the most expensive of any of the types discussed.*

Broadloom *is another term frequently misunderstood. Many people think it means plain carpeting, or that it is a special weave in itself, whereas it really refers to the width of the loom (usually 9, 12, or 15 feet). Therefore any of the carpet weaves above may be broadloom, whether they are plain or patterned.*

A good carpet or rug deserves good care. Protect it from beneath with a pad, from above with frequent cleanings. A soiled carpet or rug wears out much faster than one that is kept clean.

By all means, send your carpets and rugs to a professional carpet cleaner to remove embedded oily soil that a vacuum cleaner does not remove. Wall-to-wall carpeting can be cleaned in your home.

HAND-MADE CARPETS AND RUGS

Some of the best hand-made rugs and carpets are made in this country, while others are imported; all are more expensive than their machine-made counterparts. You will find beautiful Alpujarra rugs from Spain, peasantlike in feeling, with simple, stylized, and geometric designs. Or there are traditional floral carpets from Scotland and England, handsome French Aubusson and Savonnerie rugs, and well-styled contemporary designs.

Other imported hand-made rugs come from Puerto Rico, North Africa, Sweden, and from other parts of the world. Then there are Persian orientals, made to American specifications.

When you choose a new carpet or rug, be sure to consider just what kind of wear it will have to withstand. Rooms where the traffic is heaviest should always have carpets or rugs of the best quality. If you have to economize, use less expensive carpeting in rooms where the family spends less time. Above all, beware of so-called bargains and buy from a reliable dealer.

HARD FLOORING

Hard-surface floorings are now available in a wide variety of textures, patterns, and colors. Though handsome wood floors are always in good taste, rubber tile, asphalt, linoleum, vinyl, and cork floorings also make smart and serviceable floors. If you want a really dramatic floor, rubber tile or vinyl floorings can be laid in intricate patterns (geometric designs or blending stripes), or metal strips and metal motifs will give a dramatic touch to wood or composition flooring. Asphalt tile makes a sturdy floor, and has an additional advantage in that it is possible to install it directly on cement slab without a subfloor. Cork also makes a good flooring because it is resilient and keeps noise at a minimum. Or you can use such natural materials as polished brick, stone, or slate; little upkeep is involved since they need only periodic waxing.

Asphalt and vinyl asbestos tile are recommended for almost any room in the house. Cork is recommended except for kitchens and basement rooms, and rubber, solid vinyl, and cushion-back vinyl tile for all except basement rooms.

▲ *A bold geometric design makes a really dramatic and serviceable flooring and adds pattern to this otherwise plain traditional hall. Carpeting makes the stairs safer than leaving them bare.*

PAINT

There are several different types of paint: the usual oil-base paint (both flat and enamel), lacquer, rubber-base paint, and various water-emulsion paints. Both rubber-base and oil-base paints come in flat, semigloss, and glossy finishes. Lacquers provide a high gloss and are resistant to most liquids.

If you are doing your own painting, buy good quality paints; and before you decide on a particular paint color, ask your paint dealer for chips of various shades to try in the room to be painted. Look at the chips both in daylight and under artificial light. But remember that all colors, except very light ones, will look a shade or two darker on the wall. Even if you choose a standard color, it's a good idea to have your dealer mix the paint in his mixing machine to be sure there is no deposit on the bottom of the can.

Putting a few drops of wall color in the white ceiling paint will make your ceiling color blend better with the walls than would a stark white ceiling.

303

It is extremely difficult to achieve perfect effect by painting over old wallpaper. Seams may show, and it is impossible to mask the pattern in an embossed paper. However, if you are willing to settle for results that are not flawless, a lot of labor can be saved by painting over the wallpaper. If you decide to do this, be sure that any loose parts of the paper have been pasted back on the wall.

WALLPAPER

New designs, textures, and finishes have expanded the uses of wallpapers these days. Because most of them are washable (and some are coated so they are actually scrubbable) you can use them in bathrooms, kitchens, and other places where the wear might be heavy. Wallpapers add warmth and interest to your walls and can act as a contrast to plain painted walls; also a patterned paper can often disguise poor architectural details. If your furnishings are sparse, papered walls tend to give the room a "furnished" feeling. Likewise, papering a too-high ceiling will tend to make it seem lower.

When you shop for wallpapers, take home samples that are large enough to pin on the wall and live with for a day or. so. Look at them in daylight and by artificial light, and consider the scale of the pattern in relation to the size of your room and the other things you have.

For your convenience if you plan to hang the paper yourself, many of the wallpaper manufacturers include a "how-to-hang" slip in each roll of paper. Also there are attractive ready-pasted wallpapers that are easy to hang.

▲ *A simple bamboo wallpaper design adds a distinctive note to this contemporary room with an oriental feeling.*

Index

Good Housekeeping	is indebted to the following photographers and decorators for permission to use material included in this book

PHOTOGRAPHERS

Alderman Studios
Morley Baer
Paul Berg
Edward Bourdon
Brand Studios
William Branham
Ernest Braun
Robert Cleveland
Pat Coffey
Dearborn-Massar
Edgar de Evia
Fassett
Richard Garrison
Frank Gaynor
George de Gennaro
Leslie Gill
Gottscho-Schleisner

Pedro E. Guerrero
Gordon Ham
Wendy Hilty
William Howland
Bill Jackson
Bill Jarrett
Lee Jenks
Ted Koepper
Rudolph E. Leppert
Ulric Meisel
Michael Miller
Rodney Morgan
Florian de Narde
Paul D'Ome Studios
Maynard Parker
Charles Pearson
George Peterson

Dale Rooks
Ben Rose
Ben Schnall
Julius Shulman
Richard A. Smith
Ben Somoroff
Stone & Steccati
Roger Sturtevant
George Szanik
Max Tatch
Hans Van Nes
Nowell Ward
Martin Weber
Stuart Weiner
Hi Williams

DECORATORS

John Abbate
Elizabeth Abrams
Ethyl Alper
Bob Anderson
Catherine Armstrong
Justin Beauchat
Brewster Board
Dora Brahms
John and Earline Brice
Phoebe Broido
Bob Brown
Everett Brown
George Brown
Yale Burge
John P. Burns
R. L. Byrd
Jack Cameron
Le Roy Chambers
Alice Charles
Harbine Chatfield
Jack Conner
John Courtney
Bert Curtin
Andre Fiber
Harry E. Francis
Jeanne Frank
Don Garnier
Don Glaser
John Greer

Michael Greer
Stanley Haggart
Florence Hayward
James G. Hendrix
Donald Hess
Marion Heuer
Jack Ingraham
Barbara Joseloff
Melanie Kahane
Marge Kane
Lynn Kelly
Madge Kennedy
Haygood Laseter
The Lehmans
Kenneth Lind
Mimi S. Livingstone
Lubliner & Himmel
Mary T. Luscher
Ellen Lehman McCluskey
Paul McCobb
Mallory & Tillis
Manashaw & Daggett
Aline Mann
Gladys Miller
Minka
Jack Navin
William Pahlmann
Al Parker

Don Pelham
Lois Faye Reed
Sylvia Reed
Beverly Reitz
Mary Ritter
Jacuelyn Ross
Susan Ross
Gertrude Ruben
Tina Ruvel
Laurine Sands
Marcella Schwarb
Shaw & Draper
Louis de Haven Shaw
Donn M. Sheets
Blair L. Smith
James Merrick Smith
C. Eugene Stephenson
William Stephenson
Myrtle Todes
Kenneth Volz
Sherle Wagner
Maurice Weir
Harvey Welch
Beatrice West
Anne Winkler
John Wornok
Otto Zenke